ABOUT THE INSTITUTE OF SALES PROMOTION

The Institute of Sales Promotion (ISP) is the industry body that represents the sales promotion industry in its broadest sense, with membership drawn from both promoters and their agencies as well as the supplier companies that service this important sector of the marketing industry. The ISP's purpose is to promote, progress and protect professional and effective sales promotion and it does this by:

- promoting sales promotion and its benefits to organizations and to the regulatory authorities;
- progressing the achievement of excellence in promotional marketing by educating all parties in best practice and in the effectiveness and versatility of sales promotion;
- protecting stakeholders' interests in using sales promotion as part of their sales and marketing activity through the provision of a Legal Advisory Service and by promoting responsible self-regulation in line with the CAP code.

In 2005 the **ISP Motivation Diploma** was launched, a course and qualification specifically designed for the motivation industry, and this book forms a key part of the course material. John Fisher has also been a member of the team that developed the course and a central figure in devising its content.

For details of this course, or the ISP's Diploma and Certificate courses in Promotional Marketing, please visit www.isp.org.uk.

"We are very pleased to endorse this book as it forms an essential part of our Motivation Diploma course. John's understanding of the motivation industry has been invaluable to us and this book is a testament to his experience and expertise."

Chris Bestley, ISP Education Consultant

HOW TO RUN SUCCESSFUL INCENTIVE SCHEMES

THIRD EDITION

JOHN G FISHER

**KOGAN
PAGE**

London and Sterling, VA

Publisher's note

Every possible effort has been made to ensure that the information contained in this book is accurate at the time of going to press, and the publishers and author cannot accept responsibility for any errors or omissions, however caused. No responsibility for loss or damage occasioned to any person acting, or refraining from action, as a result of the material in this publication can be accepted by the editor, the publisher or the author.

First published in 1995 by Kogan Page Limited as *A Manager's Guide to Staff Incentives and Performance Improvement Techniques*
Second edition published in 2000 as *How to Run Successful Incentive Schemes*
Third edition published in 2005

120 Pentonville Road
London N1 9JN
United Kingdom
www.kogan-page.co.uk

22883 Quicksilver Drive
Sterling VA 20166-2012
USA

© John G Fisher, 1995, 2000, 2005

The right of John G Fisher to be identified as the author of this work has been asserted by him in accordance with the Copyright, Designs and Patents Act 1988.

ISBN 0 7494 4396 0

British Library Cataloguing-in-Publication Data

A CIP record for this book is available from the British Library.

Library of Congress Cataloging-in-Publication Data

Fisher, John G.
How to run successful incentive schemes/John Fisher -- 3rd ed.
    p. cm.
"First published as A Manager's guide to staff incentives and performance improvement techniques in 1995."
    Includes index.
    ISBN 0-7494-4396-0
    1. Employee motivation. 2. Incentives in industry. I. Fisher, John G.
Manager's guide to staff incentives and performance improvement techniques. II. Title.
    HF5549.5.M63M57 2005
    658.3'142--dc22

                              2005009394

Typeset by Datamatics Technologies Ltd, Mumbai, India
Printed and bound in Great Britain by Creative Print and Design (Wales), Ebbw Vale

Contents

Preface to the third edition

It would be impossible to thank everyone by name in the writing of this third edition but some organizations and their clients deserve specific credit for allowing me to write about their particular experiences. They are: BI Inc (USA), Everest Conseil (France), IDS (UK), Indesit (UK), Motivano (UK) and P&MM (UK). There have been considerable advances in internet communication between businesses in the last five years and I have reflected this in my updated chapters on vouchers, merchandise and measuring performance. In addition, the vast arena of employee benefits has changed out of all recognition thanks to some exciting developments in interactive software and the introduction of company intranets. The revised chapter on flexible benefits attempts to cover the latest ground in this important area.

Finally I would like to thank John Sylvester, P&MM and Mark Carman, Motivano, Jeanne Steward, Akadine Research and Mike Kealey, Kealey HR for specific help on some key case histories, without which the new edition would be much the poorer.

1

The profit potential

Most people exert only 15 per cent of their combined intelligence, skills and aptitudes in their employment.

William James

IMPROVING PERFORMANCE

The corporate goal of every organization is to survive. If it can make a profit or create a surplus at the same time, even better. But a corporate entity by itself does not make profits. People do. The sum total of all the employees' efforts and the efforts of distributors creates the wealth which allows the company to invest in new systems, products and services for its future survival. So doing business in the long term is the process of people improving their performance at work.

But how many employees ever reach their potential at their place of work? Almost everyone has the capacity to perform better, whether they produce documents, deliver services or create company policy. Individual one-to-one coaching can help, but the most cost-effective solution is a group performance improvement programme, whether for 50 or 5,000 participants. Increasingly such schemes now operate across language barriers and country borders with relative ease, thanks to the internet.

While rewriting this third edition of *How to Run Successful Incentive Schemes* I was very conscious how much has changed and how much has stayed the same in the five years since the last edition. The most obvious changes have been to do with business-to-business communication, both internally and externally. Thanks to software application developments most businesses these days talk to each other by e-mail with attachments. Many organizations have invented their own intranets and private websites so that specific, confidential communication can take place, whether that is between staff, between buyers and sellers or between manufacturers and distributors. You will find some good examples in the chapters about flexible benefits and rewards. In addition within the business community we have become much less nationalistic and parochial. Many programmes are now run cross-border in several languages. Most employees these days have direct contact with their colleagues in other countries and often in other continents, so understanding what makes other nationalities tick is increasingly becoming as important as mastering your own work culture.

What has not changed at all has been the fundamental opportunity to tap into every human being's latent behavioural drives to improve the way he or she does things. The more research we uncover, the more compelling are the reasons for introducing so-called performance improvement programmes.

The regular use of individual or group performance improvement programmes can help you identify what your current operating standards are, how your organization really functions and what capacity for improvement there might be. You can then improve those standards through specific training, better internal communication, regular feedback and appropriate rewards to create incremental benefits at every level in the business. Improving performance is the goal of most organizations today, where being better at what you do is just as important as getting bigger. But do these programmes work?

Volvo

Volvo UK was concerned about the diminishing returns it was achieving using cash sums for dealers as an incentive to sell automobiles. It was two years away from being able to introduce a replacement model for the then-mature 300 series small car, but it still needed sales now.

It was decided that a mixture of cash and non-cash incentives should be used for the first time to stimulate sales. Dealers were given a specific target with mid-campaign awards of luxury Orient Express baggage. Fifty top dealers were to be rewarded with a lavish incentive trip on the Venice–Simplon Orient Express with two further nights in Venice, staying at the Danieli Hotel. Salespeople received a selection of retail vouchers for each car sold.

The results were astounding. Market share for the second quarter leapt from 2.66 per cent on the previous year to 4.75 per cent, giving the importers, Lex Service plc, a 23 per cent increase in imported units over the previous year. The performance improvement was reported prominently in the *Financial Times* under the heading, 'Incentives help Volvo reach record sales'.

Lucent Technologies

Lucent Technologies introduced an incentive programme for all employees called 'It's All About ME'. ME is the internal acronym for the Microelectronics division in the United States. The scheme was designed to increase employee recognition, generate cost-savings and create revenue-generating ideas. Participants received points for being recognized by a peer, while a manager did so for being a top achiever in any given quarter. They could also earn points by submitting cost-saving or revenue-generating ideas. Points could be redeemed for items in a reward catalogue which included individual travel. The entire programme was funded from the savings and revenues created from the scheme itself.

Over 54 per cent of the entire workforce participated, producing 6,000 ideas, of which 2,100 were approved for implementation in such areas as recycling scrap, reducing the cost of overnight mail, improving plant safety and making e-mail more efficient. During the first year of the programme £13 million (US~$20 million) worth of cost savings and new revenue were accumulated as a direct result of 'It's All About ME'.

SNCF (French Railways)

SNCF – the national French railway system – needed to introduce confident usage of its customer ticketing system (SOCRATES), and at the same time to instil the idea in over 7,000 employees that making sales and keeping customers was important. It was decided after extensive analysis that 30 per cent of performance should be knowledge based, with the remaining 70 per cent based on sales. Nine key objectives were isolated, on which comic strip training modules were based (starting a conversation, talking to clients while using the system, deciding the best ticket option, offering discounts where appropriate). The awards were based on merchandise by mail order or a choice of retail vouchers for successful attainment of leagued thresholds across 23 separate rail regions in France. There were three levels of reward in each of the three categories of home, leisure and hi-fi/video, totalling 93 specific items presented in a loose-leaf catalogue format.

Sales volume increased significantly in all regions, but of more importance with such a long-term investment was the considerable and identifiable improvement in technical fluency of the staff with the new ticketing system.

IBM

IBM's eServer division was in the throes of launching the next generation of server products and needed the positive support and endorsement of its third party resellers. The existing incentive scheme had just 600 registered participants and was largely based on sending printed material through the mail. An internet-linked invitation process produced a 250 per cent increase in registered participants, bringing the total participant database to 1,500 at a fraction of the cost of recruiting participants by mail.

The revised Circle of Success website included hyperlinks to other IBM sites so that participants could access detailed product information just when they needed it. Participants earned points for every sale made during the year, and these could be allocated to individuals or pooled for distribution to the whole reseller business. Specific points were offered each quarter for xSeries products sold, and all points were credited within 48 hours and posted on the website. An increase of 42 per cent in sales to this channel was recorded, with the added benefit of a much wider base of participants, creating a firm platform for future promotions.

AA

The Automobile Association in the United Kingdom responds to members, calls when they break down on the UK's roads, as well as offering many other automotive-related services. Acquiring new members helps the organization to maintain lower service costs, and is vital for its long-term development. The AA employs over 14,000 staff who are all encouraged to attract new members and sell other AA services whenever they can, even if recruiting new members is not a core job role.

The Qdos points scheme offered all participants a range of vouchers, merchandise, travel and leisure products in return for registering new member and product leads to the sales team. The leads generation programme has helped to achieve a cost per acquired customer of less than £6 (US $10), which is much less expensive than advertising or direct mail or indeed any other promotional recruitment channel.

WHERE SHOULD YOU BEGIN?

● **Offer more money.** You could take this option, but as you will see later, money is an expensive way to incentivize or reward behavioural change. Offering more money may change the speed at which people work but it does not, in isolation, solve the problem of lack of focus or inefficient working practices. Nor does it instil sincere, long-term loyalty.

- **Provide stock options.** You could offer stock options for improved company performance, but it takes time for the figures to be generated and there may be little correlation between an ordinary individual's performance and the success of the corporation as a whole. There is also strong evidence that performance-related pay for senior managers is often randomly awarded and fails to promote lasting organizational improvement.
- **Provide non-cash rewards.** You could decide to offer one-off awards for specific performance improvement. But what should the awards be? A trophy? A certificate? More luncheon vouchers? A set of luggage? A meal for two? Or even a weekend in Paris? If you decide to reward one department or one grade of employee, what about all the others?
- **Provide travel.** Incentive travel is by far the most popular non-cash incentive, as perceived by participants. Companies that earmark a budget for incentives regularly spend considerable sums on overseas incentive travel. The UK estimate for 2004 was £800 million (US $1,300 million). In the United States, industry estimates are as high as £4,000 million (US $6,400 million). Is this the most effective use of any given budget? Do participants actually work harder or are you simply rewarding the predictable top echelon? Even if you are convinced it works, how should you decide which venue to choose, what kind of programme to run once you get there, and how to make the most efficient use of hotels, airlines and all the other supplier services that are part of the incentive travel experience?
- **Provide goods and services.** Perhaps a range of merchandise would be more suitable, or better still, store vouchers so that winners can choose what they want. With the move towards more personal freedom in all walks of life, perhaps some system of electronic credit on a smart card might be more appropriate.

- **Provide better training.** We know from employee surveys and research that staff value acquiring new skills and like to be rewarded for putting those skills into practice, so perhaps a scheme to offer more training would be appropriate?
- **Recognition systems.** Then there is always the question of recognition, not only for specific achievements during the year, but for consistently high performance over the full year or even over the length of a career in the form of long-service awards. Are such items effective? What is the best way to use them in a complex company where people may perform a wide range of different functions?
- **Change your processes.** Improving the way individuals go about their everyday tasks will certainly improve personal motivation, but in isolation it could be perceived as change for change's sake. Should people be rewarded simply for doing their job a little bit differently?

Measuring performance standards

Most important of all is the question of setting standards and monitoring individual performance. Within a sales environment it is relatively easy to track sales performance. But with the increasing emphasis on quality and consumer accountability, what quality measures could you introduce for staff to provide the correct cocktail of checks and balances? What about staff who apparently have no output? Once measures are defined, you need to set up systems to monitor progress. Sometimes the cost of monitoring may outweigh the estimated financial benefits of higher performance, so how can you refine the scheme to deliver a balanced result and a bottom-line, incremental return on investment (ROI)?

Deciding what to invest

Deciding what represents an appropriate budget to promote performance improvement is a discipline in itself. Many industries set themselves a percentage of turnover. Others set a fixed budget. Some calculate a percentage of employees' take-home pay. However, the most efficient way to set a budget is based on the incremental profit or benefit the additional activity will generate. The assumptions and estimates will be different for each situation, even within the same company. To start the whole process off, you need to identify an overall financial or process improvement aim, so that the fixed costs of promoting the process change are appropriate to the variable cost of achieving the improvement. In some situations you may decide no amount of money will ever change the outcome significantly.

Bearing in mind all these problems and the variable nature of the choices that can be made, is it all worth it?

SPECIFIC INCREMENTAL PROFIT

Experience with clients new to performance improvement and those who have been using motivation programmes for many years shows that identifiable additional profits are generated. But no single technique works in isolation. Often, the true benefits come from synergy: sales working with support staff; separate subsidiaries sharing a common database; tailored schemes for junior and senior staff; layered incentives for different levels; the development of new communication channels; better administrative processes. Companies that use many or all of the techniques in this book have done so for some time and will continue to do so in the future for as long as they can show an additional benefit to both shareholders and employees.

Within the performance improvement area one thing is certain. A business will not improve until the performance of the people it employs improves. The challenge is to unlock that potential for the organization's benefit and create job roles that are more fulfilling.

The additional profit potential is enormous. Almost all companies claim they undertake some type of performance improvement activity. From the small collection of published case histories and anecdotal evidence I have collected over the years, improvement can represent additional turnover of anywhere between 5 and 50 per cent, sometimes even more, for a minimal outlay.

These techniques should not only be applied to the business world. A few years ago Professor Michael Barber of Keele University released the results of a survey of attitudes among 10,000 young people at school. It revealed a general lack of motivation among 40 per cent of pupils, with up to 20 per cent of 16-year-olds truanting regularly. Between 30 and 40 per cent claimed they would rather not go to school. In the same sample 70 per cent said they counted the minutes to the end of most lessons. This waste of young, human potential to improve is enormous.

This guide is intended to help managers and supervisors tap into the vast human resource within their organization and beyond, and exploit the natural desire humans all share for improvement. Few people deliberately set out to perform poorly at work. But as William James discovered in the 19th century, most people use less than 15 per cent of their talents for their employer's benefit or for the good of their organization. With the right environment, in the 21st century, developing a 'performance improvement' culture could help foster a significantly improved contribution, and a more empowered and enthusiastic workforce in the future.

SUMMARY

- Most employees have the capacity to improve their performance.
- There are many examples of incremental profit using performance improvement techniques.
- Incentives range from cash, options and vouchers to merchandise, travel and even recognition for a job well done.
- The true benefits come from synergy between participating groups or departments.
- Developing a performance improvement culture is the key to a more productive workforce.

2 The human audit

The answer is not separate from the problem.

Krishnamurti

A performance improvement programme cannot be built on the basis of a few chance conversations and a hundred sets of luggage. If it could, improving performance would be much easier and much more common. You need to consider in great detail who you are trying to motivate, how they operate within the wider context of the company, how the business performs within its market sector and what practical measures can be put in place to monitor performance. A programme which costs more than the incremental benefit it is designed to achieve is of no practical value to an organization.

But research, in motivation terms, is not about anonymous participants. You start with what you know, namely your own industry, your own company history, your own people, your own objectives. It is going to mean a considerable commitment of time spent at head office and around the branches or local offices rummaging through personnel files, sales records, commission statements, historical company performance records, and asking specific people a few important questions. Inevitably you will find that the vital pieces of information are missing or have never been collected in the way you want them. You will get considerable resistance from every department, since people will at first be suspicious of your intentions. After all, why bother to investigate motivation when everyone knows that money is the only thing that motivates people to work harder? (See Chapter 5 to find out if it does.)

But before you start collecting data, consider carefully whether what you are collecting will be relevant when you come to assess opportunities for performance improvement. Here are some research guidelines which will be useful, but there may be other records relevant to your company situation. Leave no stone unturned.

Research principles

Most developed countries have a standard code of practice when it comes to consumer research. After all, there is usually a lot of investment at stake when a new product is developed, so reducing your risk by undertaking sensible research is the norm rather than the exception. The same goes for performance improvement schemes and incentive programmes. In general the investment can be relatively large, especially if the programme is going to be rolled out across several divisions or even to several countries, so doing detailed research will pay off.

The research process normally breaks down into these eight stages:

1. Identify the item (the participant database, last year's scheme, organizational morale, and so on).
2. Create the research design.
3. Choose the appropriate methodology (telephone, e-mail, letter, focus groups).
4. Select a meaningful sample.
5. Collect the data.
6. Analyse the data.

7. Present the data (internally to the management team, to the participants, to the sponsor).
8. Follow up (with an action plan or a revised scheme).

In addition assuring the anonymity of the respondents will not only boost participation but encourage more honest replies. The research should also be timely if it relates to past activity. It is very difficult to give an opinion about an activity which might have taken place a year or more ago.

Bearing these stages in mind, you need to build the Human Audit from big concepts down to specific detail. You could start with an overall picture of the industry you are in and the context in which your organization operates.

HUMAN AUDIT GUIDELINES

1. Analyse company performance over the previous five years in terms of sales, profits and return on investment. Pay particular attention to any mergers, acquisitions, legislation or economic factors which could have seriously affected the overall bottom-line position. It does not need to be an exhaustive financial assessment or 100 per cent accurate. You're trying to get a broad snapshot of growth, stasis or decline, both in isolation and against the background of your industry. You may need to do this by division or by product group. The marketing function is a good place to start to find this data.
2. Classify and quantify what personnel you have, and summarize their impact on company growth. It is important to clarify, perhaps for the first time, each group's strategic task and value to the company, and to describe those tasks in simple language.
3. Within the sales function identify the distribution of sales per salesperson, month by month – to get the cyclical pattern – and the overall distribution of individual performance (10 per cent above £50,000, 25 per cent below £20,000, and so on). Drawing a distribution graph of performance helps.
4. Within the administrative function, clarify any objective measures of performance, such as retention rates, absenteeism

throughput and any skill requirements you think could be improved on, given the current recruitment policy or local job market. You may also wish to consider overhead costs as a percentage of revenue to see which way the trend is leading.

5. Catalogue all previous attempts at 'motivating' any teams or groups of divisions of the company, together with any data on improved performance, accurate or spurious. Include so-called 'soft' campaigns such as suggestion schemes and staff social events.

6. Talk to all department heads in general terms about morale, motivation, performance standards and incentives, with the aim of agreeing a broad statement of the prevailing views. What they perceive to be the current state of play is more useful than what they feel ought to be the case.

When this is done, you will be in a position to do some reliable, objective research. Then and only then can you start planning the programme.

COMPANY PERFORMANCE

Let's go back a few steps. It is not your job to make a full marketing analysis of the industry or your own performance in it. If your company is well established, such a report probably exists already. The watchword is simplicity. The sort of measures you should be looking for are:

- turnover, earnings (sales);
- net profit (before tax);
- return on investment;
- inflation/interest rates in the economy;
- industry growth/decline rates;
- product trends/market take-up of new products.

The result will be a general statement of the health of the industry and your company's performance within that industry. This will be the background to the need for better motivation or, at the very least, the cultural acceptability that higher performance could make a difference. You need to be honest about the current culture before taking the project even to the stage of initial field research. Big companies are full of project teams designing apples when what the directors want is oranges or pears – or to get out of market gardening altogether. Your research will help to isolate the main barriers to higher individual and team performance.

Senior management attitudes

The attitude of the key directors in the company cannot be overstated. If your organization has never been involved in a centralized motivation programme, the idea of starting one may be perceived as a significant financial risk, which means you will need the enthusiastic support of the company 'power brokers', particularly the financial director, who, if the budgets are significant, needs to buy into the incremental benefit argument to defend any scaling down of the initial investment.

In a CBI (Confederation of British Industry) survey 70 chief executives identified staff morale and motivation to be one of four significant factors in the success of their business. So you need support from the head of the business, from the head of sales, from human resources and from the financial function. It is likely that you will be asking for up to 10 per cent of the post-tax remuneration budget to create the programme, so you need friends in high places to agree those kinds of resources.

But you also need to be honest about whether introducing fully measured performance improvement systems will reap the rewards you expect. Traditionally, in the United States and Europe, motivation schemes have been used on a consistent basis by relatively few predictable industry sectors. A leading British firm of accountants conducted a research exercise for EIBTM (European Incentive and Business Travel Meeting), covering global trends in the use of incentive travel. One section dealt with which industry is most likely to buy incentive schemes or motivation programmes, on a consistent and regular basis. The answer is in Table 2.1.

Table 2.1 Who uses incentives?

Type	% of respondents
Pharmaceuticals	10
Financial services (including insurance companies)	10
Cars	10
Automotive parts	9
Computing	9
Toiletries/cosmetics	9
Electronics	8
Electrical appliances	7
Office equipment	6
Farm equipment	5
Retail	5
Building materials	5
Heating/air conditioning	4
Leisure/catering	1
Other	2

Source: EIBTM.

I quote this not to suggest that no other sector considers performance improvement as a means to increased efficiency. Others do. But from my own experience, very few companies that are not in the sectors listed in the table use performance improvement on a regular, planned basis. The relatively low use by the retail sector of staff motivation schemes is perhaps one reason why the customer service reputation of many retail personnel is so poor. One element is clearly the margin in the product. Automotives, pharmaceuticals, computers and life insurance all benefit from a high margin, thereby making it possible to invest more of the accrued profit for long-term investment in staff who can create repeat purchase and word-of-mouth recommendations.

Things do change over the years. For years banks have had a fearsome reputation for adopting a master–servant approach to customer service. But in recent times enormous resources have been ploughed back into the customer relationship, as the banks began to realize that no one stays with one bank for life any more, particularly with the advent of internet banking. As in most industries, the response has been forced upon them by fierce competition, the general growth in consumer awareness and freedom of choice. By voting with their feet, consumers have forced the banks into a radical rethink of their customer relationships. That means looking carefully at staff performance when they come into contact with customers.

If you are in an industry that does not currently use performance improvement techniques on a regular basis, you may have to work a little harder than your counterpart in the automotive industry or the financial services sector to establish a sound cost/benefit analysis. This is one reason why a thorough appraisal of current top-level attitudes within the organization is so necessary.

PERSONNEL INVENTORY

The next task is a detailed analysis of the personnel you intend to motivate. How many are there? Are they employed, self-employed, franchisees, part-time? What profile is each group or subgroup? Do you consider the profile differences to be significant in terms of motivation? Age? Sex? Length of service? Grade or status within their group? Current earnings?

Issues to consider about sales networks

Table 2.2 gives an example of a personnel survey for an automotive company and a pharmaceutical company. They are both involved in sales to a lesser or greater degree.

You will see from the comparison that a scheme to motivate one group may not be appropriate for the other group. But avoid thinking of solutions at this stage. You need to concentrate on the analysis so that their primary job functions come into sharp focus.

Table 2.2 Two salesforce profiles

	Automotive dealer principals	Pharmaceutical representatives
Number	300	45
Age range	Average 49	Average 31
Sex	95% male	55% female
Education	Secondary	Degree, PhD
Location	National	South only
Status	Franchisee principals	Employed consultants
Service	20 years average	4 years average
Earnings	£50–150,000, average £70,000	£40–60,000

Strategic role

You should then state the strategic role of each group within the business. We can all agree that new business has an important part to play in the ongoing viability of a company, but what proportion should it represent? For example, in some industries repeat business can be as high as 90 per cent, so the role of the salesforce may be largely representation to existing clients. In other industries, new business can be as high as 40 or 50 per cent of total sales turnover. In this case the performance improvement plan needs to reflect this requirement to generate new sales each year from new or existing customers.

Retention

You may need to look at projected retention rates for specific work groups, especially if the industry has in the past operated on relatively high recruitment/low retention ratios. Whatever scheme you eventually devise could be very different if you discover that in any 12-month period 50 per cent of those who start the period do not make it to the end of your performance cycle. More importantly, what about all the new people who have joined since the programme started? How will they be incorporated and at what level of reward or measurement? Should they even be included? If not, how will their job performance be affected if they are excluded indefinitely from an incentive or reward programme? Should you set minimum qualifying limits for new staff?

Distribution

You may have several categories of sales distribution working in a complementary manner. Financial services is a good example of this. A bank, for example, might have its own direct sales force selling cold to new prospects or warm to introduced leads from its branch network. It might also have an advisory arm which sells products to independent intermediaries (brokers). Or it might have staff within branches who take the initial enquiry and qualify it for other salespeople to follow up and convert, depending on the products being offered or the current legislation of financial services. Each distribution arm needs a specific approach when it comes to performance improvement.

Representatives

Within the automotive industry, there will be salespeople with franchised dealerships but also an employed field or zone sales force who market the manufacturer's package of products and services to the franchisees. They can be a vital part of the motivational mix as they are often the front line for the manufacturer when it comes to promotion and acceptability of the programme. (They are also invaluable in providing relevant streetwise feedback on whether the scheme is working the way you want it to work, and on which dealerships are not participating.)

Tracking sales

Most businesses have some cyclical trend. Peak month for pension sales is just before the end of the tax year. Toy sales peak in December. Knowledge of the peaks as well as the troughs can determine not only when to launch the programme but when to boost any reward credits in the scheme and when to cut back. In complex business-to-business situations, such as the completion of a large IT (information technology) system sale to a multinational, you need to decide at what moment you perceive the sale to have been made so you can confirm a fair allocation of the credit due. You may even decide with some types of contract sales that credit is minimal, because the sale is often a company team effort led from the very top. So credit is given for opening the door or the quality of the process which resulted in the contract, rather than the eventual income generated from the sale itself.

Profile and geographic distribution

You need to analyse what proportion of the sales force brings in the bulk of the sales, split between existing and new if relevant. In other words, does the 80/20 rule (where 80 per cent of sales are produced by 20 per cent of the people) work for you? A further sophistication could be an analysis of geographical distribution. This may reveal nothing other than a match with the general population distribution, but you might surprise yourself. One London-based life insurance company I worked with had a tremendously successful Scottish operation. To a casual observer, this could be put down to a forceful, enthusiastic regional manager. After a bit of digging, I discovered it was more due to the fact that the company was originally based in Scotland when it was founded some 50 years before, and the relatives and descendants of those early policyholders were still very much alive, kicking and paying their premiums on the dot each month.

Issues to consider about those who do not sell

People who don't sell generally tend to be more difficult to classify and analyse. With salespeople you can always look at their figures. With administrative and management groups judgement can be much more subjective about their performance or attitudes to motivation techniques. Why do you need to know anyway? Surely administrative staff are simply there to do their job? If they do, they stay; if they don't, they get fired. The problem in many companies is that they may not be performing, but still don't get fired. The waste can be calculated and is enormous, even with the most rudimentary accounting system. In practice administrative staff are usually the group that could make the biggest performance improvement of all, supporting the received wisdom (and the clinically researched truth) that given the right cultural environment, most people will strive to do better.

Strategic role

Does your organization have certain departments that have a strategic contribution to the business you operate? If you rely on your website to make contact with customers, it may be that you need to concentrate any performance improvement scheme on maintaining service standards in this area. If your main market advantage is your production capability, it would be foolish to leave manufacturing out of the performance improvement audit.

Attendance and retention

There are many tried and tested ways of dealing with staff attendance rates and retention, from cash bonuses to return interviews and negative sanctions. But society's attitudes change quickly, and what used to be behaviour to punish may well now be behaviour simply to correct. Few employees set out deliberately to build up a poor attendance record, so doing a proper audit may well be the only way to discover the hidden reasons behind bad timekeeping. The answer is rarely just more incentives. Often the whole process of measuring and reporting absenteeism will need to change if you are to see any improvement.

Retention rates may not simply be a question of what benefits you offer to instil loyalty. Deciding to stay with an organization, particularly in a market of full employment, is a complex decision, often based more on perceived opportunities within the organization than on tangible benefits. You need to dig quite deeply to discover why your overall retention rates are what they are.

Job descriptions

It has been calculated that most large organizations change their structure every two to three years. It is quite likely therefore that a number of employees will be operating with out-of-date job descriptions. With the trend towards outsourcing it is also quite likely that some fundamental parts of many jobs in large organizations will have disappeared. The human audit needs to take these changes into account and not simply assume that the description of jobs provided by the human resources department is still true in practice, as this will have a significant effect on any task-based incentive programme which may be introduced as a result of the human audit.

What types of non-sales staff are there?

- the factory or processing unit;
- clerical;
- junior executives;
- managers;
- departmental heads;
- directors.

Depending on your type of business you may even use a number of consultants who will not be employees, but will still have a strong influence on operational morale and task performance.

Analysing the profile of people in the factory or processing unit could be a never-ending task. The numbers, types of worker and the complexity of many large companies can make this job very daunting. (This is one reason that few large companies even attempt it.) But do not forget what we're looking for: a general feel for the *status quo* with some clues as to how to improve job performance in the future. Understanding what part people play in the creation of the product, including the main procedures they follow, is what you need to concentrate on.

The Tennessee Valley Authority (TVA)

The TVA is a US government-owned electric utility. With increasing competition and the need to keep existing customers satisfied, the TVA developed 'The Quality Alliance' with its key distributors, internal managers and customer service centres. In essence, the company went through a Total Quality Management programme which helped work groups to analyse their work processes and define what quality should be in their particular department. Part of the process was the development of a Customer Satisfaction Index to indicate areas for improvement in the future. In the words of the director of member and employee services, 'The Quality Alliance offers a fresh new approach to customer satisfaction as well as bringing pride and excitement back to the power distributor and its employees'.

Without a thorough understanding of what each work group does, such levers for performance improvement can never be developed.

Absenteeism/attendance

Looking at processing teams brings its own basket of typical problems which need measuring in order to decide, eventually, which ones to tackle first. Absenteeism is the most obvious symptom of poor performance, and managers in human resources will be fully aware of techniques to improve the ratio. However, although absenteeism rates overall in the developed countries have remained static at around 5 per cent over the past 10 years, less than half of employers bother to question absentees when they return to work. Very few employers reward 100 per cent attendance in the workplace. It is often a social problem in addition to a company problem. When you analyse job functions, whether the operatives are building a car or processing credit card transactions, it is clear that job enrichment has not been thought through. One reason that so many bank processing staff are part-time could be the tedious nature of the processing tasks they are asked to perform. No one could stand to do it on a full-time basis. The early 21st-century world of work is a strange mixture of Victorian monotony and futuristic data manipulation. So much is accomplished, but at what price to the minds of modern day 'mill workers'? There is much that could be organized for higher job enrichment, but until we have analysed what procedures constitute acceptable job performance, we cannot begin to change it for the better.

After absenteeism, you may look at the exit interviews. But take care not to assume everyone leaves for more money in the next town. Retention factors reveal more about the way staff are managed than the staff themselves. They are the equivalent of the supermarket checkout. Employees often take their basket of complaints about poor management with them when they leave. The remaining managers count the cost in terms of replacement and retraining.

Grievances

Another area to consider is the number of grievances brought to the supervisors or managers as a general measure of satisfaction. You have to take a view as to whether the levels are affected in any way by economic factors such as recession. People tend to complain less if they are busy and business is expanding. At this initial stage talk to the supervisors and managers on a one-to-one basis, but listen carefully. They may not be used to talking so frankly about how they feel about job performance, especially if there is any perception that you are 'spying' on their activity levels. They will be used to work study programmes and may expect you simply to set them higher productivity targets. What they will not readily recognize is any probing about motivation or ways to increase job satisfaction. You may find a fair degree of complacency, self-satisfaction, and an unwillingness to admit that the current way of organizing and rewarding work is anything other than inevitable. Collect any examples you can of procedures being done that on the face of it seem wasteful of resources or create unnecessary paperwork. Such legacies can be swept away if the analysis of job roles is carried out correctly.

Morale check

Some companies operate a regular internal morale audit to ensure that company issues such as structural changes, procedures or new products are being handled correctly by managers. This information will be useful to the performance improvement/incentives manager in highlighting specific problems.

DIGGING DEEPER

Your next task may require more devious tactics. I used to handle promotions for a direct-marketing printing company which specialized in personalized home stationery such as letterheads, labels and envelopes. The research task was to discover what made consumers order certain formats. It was a straightforward job. However, the answers coming out of the advertising agency were based on consumer response and perceived preferences for certain products. In other words, the analysis was based on what sold best. A sound way to progress, in theory.

I decided to spend a day wandering around the client's factory. In particular I was interested to talk to the team that actually fulfilled the orders and reported the figures through to the board. Holding sway was a real swashbuckling 69-year-old chum of the chairman who spent overlong on lunches with his paper merchants and was looking forward to retreating to the golf course full time once his contract was over. It did not take long to discover that he had been briefing his 'girls' to switch consumers to processes that required easier production, as he was finding the new techniques a bit of a mystery to buy in to. He would get consumers to agree to an alternative paper colour on the basis of a 5 per cent reduction. In fact, he only ever carried two of the six colours advertised because he felt it was too confusing and expensive to stock so much paper on the basis of potential future orders.

After an hour's discussion with the women who administered the orders, it transpired that whatever the advertising agency put in the ads (and they tested them mercilessly), the factory just fulfilled the orders in the same old way, and had done for years. So investigating what the actual workers said and did proved more revealing than analysing any number of sales reports and customer coupons. Within a month, the personalized stationery product was revamped, the manager put out to grass, and more clerks were taken on to respond to the demand from eager consumers wanting to use their lilac paper (with matching envelopes).

The same technique should apply when it comes to investigating previous motivation schemes. You should start with the executives who formulated the schemes and implemented them. They will undoubtedly have records of when they were, what awards were made, campaign structures and what effect they had on job performance or general morale. But you need to go beyond this. You need to talk to some long-in-the-tooth participants who will have absolute recall of any oddities or absurdities in the presentation, the rules or the reward fulfilment.

During one such investigation for a client, I discovered that one year the executive in charge of sales had completely forgotten to organize the regional lunches which were meant to be low-level rewards to the locally based administration staff for their part in a sales drive. What made it worse was the fact that he was actually in a resort hotel in Spain with the top sales qualifiers on the same day the clerical winners were expecting to sit down for a well-deserved lunch.

Even good sales figures can be misleading without talking to the actual participants. Many motivation programmes suffer from an excellent launch followed by minimal follow through. This means that invariably the programme fails to get general acceptance. More and more money is arbitrarily thrown at the campaign in the form of additional awards, to the extent that in the last month of the scheme, merely being in employment brings you some kind of credit. So the increase in performance is bought at a heavy price which is not necessarily included in the official campaign records, thereby skewing any objective assessment as to its effectiveness.

UNDERSTANDING JOB ROLES IN DETAIL

A common failing with staff schemes (as opposed to sales incentives) is a lack of research into what people's jobs are and hence what they should be measured on. We undertook an assignment for a national road and rail distribution company. They had all the latest communication technology, an enviable fleet of cars, lorries and motorbikes, and an excellent relationship with the national rail network. What they did not have was any detailed description of what their people actually did. It was true that every job holder had a job description which spelt out clearly what he or she was supposed to be doing. The reality was somewhat different.

Our task was to explain to the staff the basis of their monthly cash bonuses. An amount was added to pay cheques based on a complicated financial formula known only to the personnel department. We recommended that, rather than try to explain the formula, we should look at the process. The result was a hands-on analysis of each job holder's key tasks and an agreement to reward each aspect with specific credits. Those credits were translated into cash, with a statement showing performance achievement against the agreed minimum standards. Now that the recipients understood what they were being measured on, they could take practical steps to improve their performance and improve their cash bonus in future.

Post-programme research is unlikely to exist in most non-sales schemes. It is often the case that if no one complains, the programme is deemed to be a success. Any scheme worth doing in the first place is worth researching when it is all over. To find objective judgements on whether it worked is well-nigh impossible in the absence of any post-programme report, so you may have to take an educated guess on its impact, which is not helpful when planning future initiatives. Research does pay off. A major British life assurance company polled its sales force on incentive travel destinations for the following year's incentive scheme. The top perceived destination was Hawaii. So when Hawaii was duly revealed at the sales convention, the majority of delegates felt not only that they had had an input, but that it was a genuinely popular choice.

One illuminating truism which will undoubtedly crop up will be that the lowest paid section of staff are rarely incentivized with anything other than money, middle management are offered share options and the top salespeople go to Rio. Do not despair. By building a description of what each peer group contributes to the process you will be able to identify what element of performance to highlight and provide the most appropriate reward.

RECRUITING THE DECISION MAKERS

The final piece of the jigsaw is what the key managers or departmental heads think. Inevitably they will think you want to discuss reward levels and budgets. However, this is the least of your worries. What you want from them is their general attitude to performance improvement and efficiency. Why? Because at the implementation stage you will need their active support in order to defend the concept, communicate the details to their staff and get the budgets approved. Performance improvement requires investment.

Each departmental manager will carry some mental baggage that needs to be understood and assimilated rather than criticized. The production director is keen to become more efficient but may be less interested in paying for it. The finance director will treat the problem of morale as mathematical rather than psychological. The sales director will already be looking forward to a trip abroad next year. The computer services director will not understand why there is any need to think about performance improvement at work at all, because in time job performance may well be monitored remotely, online.

The attitudes of the more successful senior managers or directors need careful consideration. Several research studies that explored the prevalence of cash as a common motivator provided an unusual insight. Within business, successful executives tend to measure their own success in terms of personal wealth and luxury status symbols. This view is reinforced by the hierarchy above them, which is constantly pushing for higher sales, lower costs and more profits; in other words, success for senior managers is measured in money. When any performance improvement programme is discussed, there will be a tendency for senior people to consider that cash will fix the problem, in terms of higher rates of pay, target-driven bonuses or options. Research with middle-level participants shows that above a basic comfort level, cash is less effective as a means of changing behaviour than non-cash rewards, or even simply peer or public recognition for a job well done. Money, after all, is only a symbol of worth.

So you need to temper senior managers' views with an appreciation of their probable attitude to money as everyone's main motivator, and steer away from instant solutions based on providing more cash. The process of performance improvement is far more complex than simply loosening the purse strings.

Agreement to a hypothetical budget is an important bridge to cross. You may be looking at somewhere between 5 and 10 per cent of total salaries, post deductions, to make significant changes to behaviour. By anyone's standards that is a significant budget. Some companies work on a percentage of revenues, anywhere between 3 and 5 per cent, if they are heavily sales-led.

TAKING AN OVERALL VIEW

Once all the interviews have been written up, you need to take a sensible, middle-of-the-road view. By exploring all these avenues, you should be able to propose a well-reasoned argument to invest in better human efficiency. With the initial audit complete, you can move on to developing the structure and rewards to suit your company profile and the current performance problems facing the company.

If you are a seasoned 'motivational interventionist' you may have already been through this initial research process, but you should avoid simply repeating the structure of an old programme, tempting as it is. There is still a need to examine whether last year's programme worked as well as it could.

I once ran a programme for automotive aftersales people called 'The Gold Standard'. In essence it was a glossy loose-leaf catalogue incentive, based on specific achievement of turnover against a target, with a few 'quality' tasks to underpin the performance. The message from the manufacturer was to emphasize the need to sell quality as well as sell volume. One without the other would be expensive in terms of poor repeat sales, so quality was crucial. As an investment, the programme returned about 20 per cent higher sales and a corresponding increase in quality. However, during the post-programme campaign analysis we researched in detail attitudes to the campaign and asked for any suggestions for improvements. There were a number of important comments, ranging from encouraging more teamwork between different departments to specifying whether incentive tax was being paid for by the manufacturer, and whether participants could add cash to any awards claimed. It revealed that the length of the qualifying period for the programme was too short to make significant differences in ordering patterns for some business partners. We were even able to float ideas about the appropriate type of rewards and structure for the next programme, so when it came to devising the follow-up scheme, the reward solution was already in the research.

Hotpoint/Creda: a case history

After some years using relatively low-level tactical incentives, General Domestic Appliances (now the Indesit Company) in the United Kingdom decided to investigate the possible use of incentives for the engineers and support staff who worked within its Hotpoint and Creda white goods after sales service division. At the outset the company had identified that it needed to improve productivity and encourage average performers to 'do that extra bit', as one of its managers put it. In particular the company was generating more requests for calls than it could currently cope with, so it needed a mechanism to encourage existing engineers to take more calls during the working week. The senior team had agreed to a three-fold audit strategy to get the answers they needed as to whether professionally run incentives would work for their culture and current organizational structure.

The human audit would cover focus group discussions with representatives from each level of the organization. The second phase would be to measure the depth of feeling and opinion through some quantitative research. The third element would be to pilot test the scheme, or at least part of it, with a sample of the engineers to see the results. If successful, the scheme would then be rolled out to the entire workforce in the hope that the test results would be duplicated on a national scale.

Qualitative research

Seven discussion groups were carried out, four in the North and three in the South, to take account of any potential regional bias in the findings. Senior managers, area managers, field supervisors, engineers, customer care managers and telesales team leaders were invited to discuss a set number of key issues regarding the more formal introduction of incentive programmes. In all 70 personnel were invited to take part out of a total workforce of around 850.

General attitudes towards incentives

Most people were very clear what incentives were for and why organizations introduced them, but opinions were divided about whether the rewards should be cash or tangibles (goods, services, merchandise, vouchers). Their experience of incentives within Hotpoint/Creda had been somewhat negative in the past, with participants claiming that payouts were small and that they were conducted more to raise morale than to provide significant rewards. They pointed to the varied nature of each engineer's job, and argued that it would be difficult to establish a level playing field in which the opportunity to claim rewards would be fair to all. There would be some conflict between wanting to do a good job and being pressurized to move on to the next call.

Opinions about a new scheme

Some principles for a new scheme were then introduced by the researchers, and participants were invited to give their views. The scheme would need to be fair for all concerned, and all departments, including administrators, should be involved. It would have to take into account various factors as there was no 'average' engineer in terms of the factors that add up to doing a good job. Most of all, the scheme should be inclusive rather than divisive; it should encourage teamwork.

Measuring performance

The researchers then introduced a number of possible ways to measure engineer performance, such as customer satisfaction, willingness to take more calls, selling service contracts, collecting revenue, and the supervisor's assessment. Opinions were sharply divided on what constituted 'good performance'.

Reward and recognition

One thing participants all agreed on was that rewards in the past had been too low to encourage a change in behaviour. They suggested that between 5 per cent and 10 per cent of post-deductions pay would be needed to achieve this. Time off was a popular concept as a possible reward, and had been tried from time to time to encourage engineers to work weekends. As for the creation of a best practice club, recognition certificates or a hosted event to congratulate top performers, these ideas received an unenthusiastic response, even though many participants had been involved with such recognition ideas in other employment.

Barriers to introducing the perfect scheme

The discussions were rounded off with a general debate about the possible barriers to introducing the 'perfect scheme'. These were quickly identified: the scheme needed to be credible, bearing in mind the haphazard way incentives had been introduced in the past; the rules needed to be tight enough to prevent cheating, or 'working the system'; the programme needed to be fair for everyone and not favour specific groups; the administration should be simple in terms of claiming rewards due, and communication

Engineer performance...

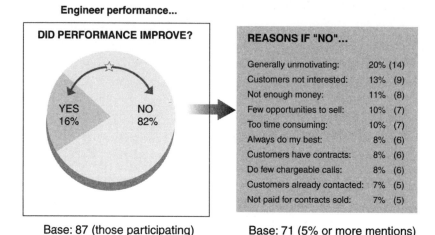

DID PERFORMANCE IMPROVE?		REASONS IF "NO"...	
YES 16%	NO 82%	Generally unmotivating:	20% (14)
		Customers not interested:	13% (9)
		Not enough money:	11% (8)
		Few opportunities to sell:	10% (7)
		Too time consuming:	10% (7)
		Always do my best:	8% (6)
		Customers have contracts:	8% (6)
		Do few chargeable calls:	8% (6)
		Customers already contacted:	7% (5)
		Not paid for contracts sold:	7% (5)

Base: 87 (those participating)   Base: 71 (5% or more mentions)

Difficult target to achieve?

Figure 2.1   Hotpoint/Creda past schemes: service contract-based

should be executed professionally and include regular updates on performance.

Quantitative research

It was clear from these discussions that a new scheme would receive a cautious welcome, but management would have to meet all the misgivings voiced in the discussions for the new scheme to be an unqualified success. A questionnaire was devised to cover the key issues arising from the discussions, and used with a sample of some 200 potential participants. In the course of a 20-minute telephone call randomly selected participants were taken through three areas of debate: past schemes, possible future schemes and ideas for communication and recognition. The sample structure included the job grade of the participant, age, rural or city, technical expertise, family status and length of service. Participants were also invited to rate the success of five types of past scheme on a scale of 'very successful' down to 'not at all successful' and asked for their reasons.

Figure 2.1 shows one example: 82 per cent of the participants declared that the 'service contract' incentive scheme (selling

Engineer performance...

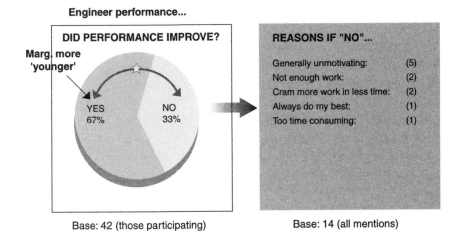

Marg. more 'younger'

DID PERFORMANCE IMPROVE?

YES 67% NO 33%

REASONS IF "NO"...

Generally unmotivating:	(5)
Not enough work:	(2)
Cram more work in less time:	(2)
Always do my best:	(1)
Too time consuming:	(1)

Base: 42 (those participating)   Base: 14 (all mentions)

Performance improved by sig. higher amount of engineers

Figure 2.2   Hotpoint/Creda past schemes: work four get paid for five

warranties to existing customers) was not successful in their eyes, because the promotion was 'generally unmotivating', the customers were not interested and the incentive amount was too low.

However, the offer to commit to working for four extra days in any month and be paid a bonus equivalent to a full day's pay scored a rating of 67 per cent as a successful incentive idea (see Figure 2.2).

Regarding future possible schemes, 61 per cent showed enthusiastic interest in a new all-embracing scheme, although they then specified that it should have rules to prevent cheating, that it should be open to all job grades, that the targets should be achievable by all grades and that the organization could not alter the scheme once launched (a reference to an earlier scheme which had been amended while it was in progress). Most favoured a monthly payout of rewards, and that cash should be the reward medium (see Figure 2.3).

As for communication and recognition, there was a general consensus that any communication is good communication, but that colleague or work-related recognition items or events would not be perceived as an attractive element of the incentive scheme.

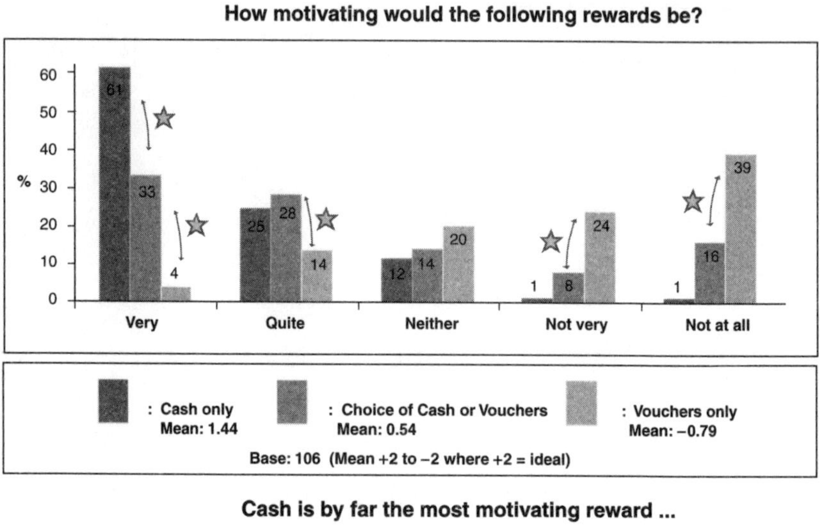

How motivating would the following rewards be?

Base: 106 (Mean +2 to −2 where +2 = ideal)

Cash is by far the most motivating reward ...

Figure 2.3 Hotpoint/Creda ideal scheme: preferred reward

Pilot test

Once the researchers were armed with all this information, a pilot test was devised to test out the strength of the proposition, the level of ideal reward, the launch technique, the ongoing communication (see Figure 2.4) and the actual level of achievement. Various tweaks were then made in preparation for the scheme being made available for a longer period across the whole engineer workforce.

TESTING YOUR PRESENTATION

If you do take the trouble to research the most recent programme, make sure you cover all the angles. The views of senior managers may not be the same as those of the staff or sales team. Communication of the detail may be clear to you if you have been living with it for the past three months, but it may not come across so clearly to junior secretarial staff or third party distributors who may only devote a fleeting few minutes to reading the brochure. It is well worth testing the

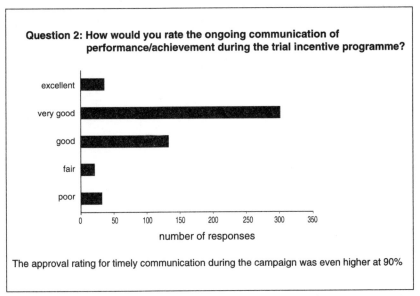

Figure 2.4   Hotpoint/Creda trial scheme: rating of communication

understanding of the campaign mechanics before going live. We once ran a national quality standards programme for a major computer manufacturer, only to discover after the first phase that head office was the only section of the participants that understood what was on offer. We changed the design to be more pictorial and less wordy. The improvement in both understanding and acceptance was significant. Never underestimate the need to keep it simple, particularly with a disparate number of job types.

There are still no guarantees. A programme devised during boom-time is unlikely to work in the middle of a recession. If quality, defined as the predictable delivery of the product to a consistent standard, is your main failing, then a volume-related sales incentive is a waste of money, time and effort. The human audit is when all these things will be found out, and it provides a bedrock for future performance improvement.

Now you have a clear view of who you are trying to motivate, you can consider what techniques may be appropriate for your participants and how an effective programme could be constructed

SUMMARY

- There are no instant solutions.
- Research each category in detail.
- Get the key decision makers involved.
- Understand fully who does what, especially administrative staff.
- Talk to the 'old timers' about past schemes.
- Do specific research of the most recent initiatives.
- Check understanding of the communication materials.

3 Constructing the programme

An axiom of virtually all the theories of motivation is that organisms strive to increase pleasure and to decrease pain.

Bernard Weiner

Scene: Top-floor office suite of a multinational petrochemical company. Board members seated around a long, polished table.

Agency Account Director: 'In conclusion, what we propose is an integrated motivation programme, targeted to particular sub-groups within the participant database, focusing on the need to appeal to both knowledge requirements and sales achievement. The result, if communicated to the degree we suggest, will enhance performance beyond the estimates laid down and produce incremental returns in excess of current budgeted expectations for the forthcoming financial year.' (Silence)

CEO: 'But where are we going?'

Agency Account Director: 'Rio.'

Most initiatives to construct a motivation programme start backwards. There is an urgency to develop the reward element in the hope that once the logistics of delivering the rewards have been arranged, performance improvement can take care of itself. In truth, sorting out the reward is the least troublesome of the tasks required to establish a profitable improvement programme. As in all marketing endeavours, establishing the objectives of the programme requires considerable thought if the expenditure is going to produce viable returns.

The human audit will have provided some clues about the most pressing objectives, but now is the time to decide which course of action to take first. This moment is usually a time of high anxiety, as various departmental managers will have differing views on what to tackle. Some will be more keen than others to press forward into action. The sales department may consider the task to be as simple as dangling a carrot in front of a donkey – and the bigger the carrot, the better. Administrative supervisors may worry about the precedent even a modest amount of discretional reward will set, and whether the internal dissemination of performance achievement will be more divisive than beneficial. At this point it may be useful to be aware of some important guidelines about what works and what does not. A round-up of motivation theory may help.

MOTIVATION THEORY

Origins

The history of motivation theory only dates back as far as Freud and Jung. The first theories revolved around the hedonistic principle that what drives most people to act in a particular way is the pursuit of pleasure and the fear of pain. However, this truism was more of an observation about human nature than a principle that could scientifically predict what a given individual or group of people would do in specific circumstances.

Clark Hull was the first to suggest some kind of general, predictive description of what motivates people. Based on the idea that behaviour is a function of an individual's inner drive and habit, he went on to establish that motivation is a function of drive, habit and incentive. Within a business context we recognize that some people appear to be 'well motivated' all the time, while others require a pattern to follow (habit) in the form of working practices and standards to perform well. A significant group only perform well when there is something in it for them (incentive).

Within the field of behavioural science, Dawkins suggests innate selfishness is also a characteristic driving force of human behaviour. 'Our genes have survived in some cases for millions of years, in a highly competitive world. This enables us to expect certain qualities in genes. This gene selfishness will usually give rise to selfishness in individual behaviour.'

Atkinson was concerned with a theory of achievement motivation, and suggested that people are driven to achieve by the conflicting tendencies to hope and fear. 'The possibility of success: the possibility of failure – the emotional conflict between hopes for success and fears of failure – individuals make a choice based on maximising personal hedonism.' In Atkinson's world achievement can be measured by calibrating the need to achieve, the probability of success and the value of the incentive being offered.

Henry Murray, in 1938, attempted to classify clinically what motivates people by categorizing human behaviour into 20 basic human needs. One of them is the need to achieve:

> To accomplish something difficult. To master, to manipulate or organise physical objects, human beings or ideas. To do this as rapidly and independently as possible. To overcome obstacles and attain a high standard. To excel one's self. To rival and surpass others. To increase self-regard by the successful exercise of talent.

Maslow's well-known theory of the hierarchy of needs (1943) goes a long way to explaining why offering higher-level incentives (lavish holidays, peer group recognition, higher personal development) is ineffective if the basic needs of the individual to have food and shelter are not first met. In other words high commission and low or nonexistent basic pay is rarely the most effective way to motivate or retain sales people, as illustrated in Figure 3.1. Arguably this triangle could also be a very useful model to constructing a multi-tiered incentive programme for

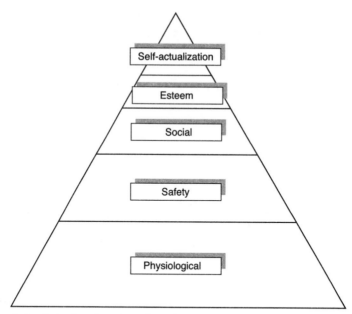

Figure 3.1 Maslow's triangle

sales people, where salaries and benefits provide basic security and the need to belong to a group, commission and non-cash incentives fulfill the need to be recognized by your peers, and the highest level describes the highest achievers who are driven by professional pride rather than rewards and are ultimately 'self-fulfilled'.

Weiner summarized various experiments concerning expectancy levels of individuals in a given task-related situation: 'In skill related tasks, expectancies tend to increase after success and decrease after failure, pointing to the importance of positive feedback when tasks are completed successfully.' So communication has a key part to play in successful incentive schemes.

Miller in 1959 proved clinically that 'the tendency to approach a goal is stronger the nearer the subject is to it'. McClelland tried to explain the rise of capitalism and entrepreneurial behaviour as a direct result of Protestantism – the reliance on individual effort rather than trust in the omnipotence of the Catholic church for guidelines on how to live in the second half of the 20th century. Fritz Heider suggested that all human behaviour

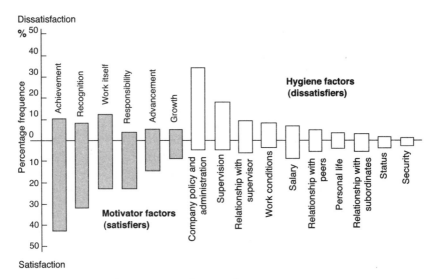

Figure 3.2   Herzberg's two-factor theory

depends on the social environment. 'When we say "he can do it", but [he] fails [to do it] only because he does not try sufficiently, then we mean that the effective personal force is smaller than the restraining environmental force ... with greater exertion he would succeed.'

Herzberg, writing in the 1950s and 1960s, contributed an important understanding of motivation in the workplace with his theory of 'satisfiers' and 'dissatisfiers'. In 1966 he set out his findings about what motivates people at work in his book *Work and the Nature of Man*. He proposed that there were two groups of factors that increased job satisfaction or decreased job dissatisfaction, but that they were not the same type of factor. The 'satisfiers' or motivators were achievement, recognition, the work itself, responsibility, advancement and personal growth. The 'dissatisfiers' or hygiene factors were organizational policy, supervision, work conditions, salary, peer relationships, personal life, subordinate relationships, status and security. (See Figure 3.2.) In practice this distinction led to 'job enrichment' programmes which attempted to improve the satisfiers and minimize the effects of the dissatisfiers. In the context of incentives and performance improvement programmes, Herzberg therefore suggests that

Table 3.1 Theorists' timeline

Date	Theorist	Issue
1901	Freud	Instinctive drives, pleasure principle
1912	Jung	Extroverts and introverts
1938	Murray	Basic human needs
1943	Maslow	Hierarchy of needs
1959	Hull	Drive theory
1964	Vroom	Motivation at work, effect of cash
1966	Herzberg	Two-factor theory
1966	Atkinson	The need for achievement
1975	Latham	Goal setting
1991	Cantor	Goals and emotions
1992	Ford	Motivational systems theory

workers are more likely to improve their performance if you include appeals to the satisfiers (recognition, responsibility, promotion prospects) rather than simply fix the dissatisfiers. For example, changing the way people are supervised or improving benefits may well improve loyalty and retention, but by itself will not motivate employees to be more productive.

A number of academics have pointed out the similarities between Maslow's need hierarchy and Herzberg's two-factor theory, in that they both suggest it is necessary to meet basic needs first before moving on to higher-level motivators. When you come to construct an appropriate incentive scheme for participants you may well need to ask the question whether this group of people can respond to enhanced satisfiers, or whether there are some basic needs that must be addressed first, such as job security and organizational attitudes to supervision.

Many other academics have endeavoured to explain common observations of human behaviour. Cottrell, in a study of social interactive behaviours in 1972, pointed to improvement in performance when people act as a group. 'When two or more people act together, the intensity of their individual behaviour often increases.'

Recent developments

In 1992 Martin Ford put forward the most comprehensive review of motivation theory to date – the Motivation Systems Theory – which gives a dozen or so guidelines on how to increase the likelihood of positive motivation in a corporate or organizational context. Put into a formula:

Achievement (job competence)
=Motivation [x] Skill [x] Responsive environment
$$\frac{}{\text{Biology}}$$

However, it has to be recognized that all the academic work of the past hundred years has been sporadic in its usefulness within a business context. Many of the principles are either just plain common sense or simply not predictive enough to be sure-fire winners when it comes to developing the structure of a motivation programme. There is no magic, scientific formula for motivating people that will ring true in every conceivable situation.

That said, there are some general principles to bear in mind when planning the structure of a sound commercial programme. By applying these principles you can lessen the possibility of failure and increase the effectiveness of your budget, but no set of principles can guarantee incremental profit. Experimentation and creativity will determine what works and what does not with a specific group of people.

Not every programme will require all of these principles, so slavish adherence to a formula will not guarantee success. You need to acquire a 'performance improvement mind-set' to guide all aspects of the programme from research to completion.

Goal setting

One important development, now widely used by commercial organizations, is a proper understanding of goal setting. In 1999 Dr Timothy McCarthy published a brief paper intended for CEOs in an attempt to pull together the accepted wisdom of how to translate goal-setting theory into practice. He reviewed the current theory as follows:

1. **Participation.** Joint goal setting between supervisors and their staff leads to higher commitment than simply telling juniors what to do.
2. **Specificity.** Goal setting can only be effective if the parameters for performance are absolutely clear.
3. **Feedback.** Regular feedback is essential in promoting a positive outcome.
4. **Challenging goals.** Objectives or targets need to be challenging if the sponsor is going to achieve a return on the investment.
5. **Commitment.** The participants must be personally committed to the goal, so the goals need to be specific to their area of influence and 'make sense'.

There is much in here that is reminiscent of Martin Ford's findings, but it is as well to have more than one reference when trying to explain to senior managers that there are indeed principles for corporate motivation which stand the test of time.

So armed with the human audit, a brief historical perspective and some basic principles of motivation, where do you go from here?

PRINCIPLES OF CORPORATE MOTIVATION

- Motivation techniques need to be applied with a sensitivity to the corporate or social environment and any other factor peculiar to the individual or group. In broad terms you need to understand 'the big picture' before proposing solutions.
- To trigger performance improvement you need to combine a goal or objective, the subject's emotions and the subject's honest assessment that improvement is possible.
- The most important characteristic of a motivation programme is the setting of a relevant goal. If you are setting more than one

goal, make sure they are not in conflict with each other. This is known as 'goal salience'.

- You must provide a method of feedback so participants can measure their performance and modify their behaviour.
- Be realistic about attainment standards and adjust them if participants are not achieving them. But continue to keep standards challenging.
- Use 'success stories' and peer group experiences to reinforce how individual performance can be improved, and recognize successful performance.
- Provide skills training so that participants have the tools to achieve higher performance.
- Create an improvement process that is gradual and incremental rather than transformational. Complete change in one step is rarely greeted with enthusiasm.
- Try several overlapping techniques over a period of time. Don't expect one idea to work for everyone all the time. Create a developing motivation strategy.
- People are complex and unpredictable. Respond to feedback as quickly as possible, keep your promises and be interested in participants' reactions. A withdrawal of participant cooperation is a failure by the motivator to understand the process.

PERFORMANCE IMPROVEMENT IN PRACTICE

Clearly the principles make good sense, but how do they translate into normal business practice? The four key elements are: research, training/skills development, communication and incentive. Each of these areas needs to be addressed if true performance improvement is to take place. In diagrammatic form, the model could look as shown in Figure 3.3, represented by the activities in Table 3.2.

The sequence begins with research of some kind, whether it is a human audit, a participant survey, competitor tracking or

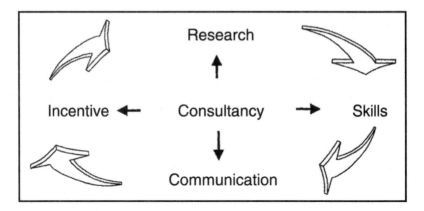

Figure 3.3 Performance improvement model

in-depth interviews. It is normal for some research to be provided by the client, but more often the 'motivational interventionist' has to identify the gaps in knowledge and undertake an
independent investigation so that a proper diagnosis of the performance issue in question can be established.

Table 3.2 List of possible components

Research	Skills	Communication	Incentive
In-house data	Distance learning	Print	Merchandise
Sector surveys	Classroom	CD ROM	Group travel
Company surveys	Intranet programmes	Intranet	Individual travel
Morale checks	Service	Conferences	Retail vouchers
In depth	Quality	Videos	Recognition items
Quality audits	Team building	Bulletins/posters	Events
Mystery shopping	Culture change	Telephone hotlines	Long service
Customer satisfaction	Attitude sessions	Team briefings	Benefits
HR exit interviews	Management supervision	Teasers	Time off

The second stage is an assessment of the skills required to do the job. Performance may be poor because the participants have never been given the training to do the new task. Skills development can take a variety of forms, from distance learning using brochures and videos to online, internet-based self-assessment and progress monitoring.

The next aspect is communication. If the problem has been correctly identified by research and participants have been given the skills to do the new task, they need to be told what the expectations are for the new task and how task achievement is to be measured. Communication could be paper or internet-based, with performance updates for each individual on a regular basis forming the backbone of the communications strategy.

Communication also covers opportunities for recognition of outstanding performance and acknowledgement of the relevant milestones being achieved. It could be argued that there should be an additional box called 'measurement' within the model, as tracking performance is not the same as initial research or setting the standard for desired performance. However, measurement is inextricably linked to communication and is part of the communication process (otherwise you would have no results to communicate), so it has not been isolated in the model as an additional section.

Finally, you need to tackle the issue of incentive or reward. You need to make a careful assessment of what kind of incentive would be appropriate to your participant database. For a group that has never taken part in a non-cash performance improvement programme before, the value of awards could be relatively small and they could be based on recognition items. For sophisticated incentive participants, travel in its many guises may be the answer. Often the solution is a combination of several types of reward.

Sitting at the heart of any effective improvement programme is the consultative element which can be brought to bear during any of the four stages when deciding on particular techniques. Each corporate situation brings its own challenges, and the advice may be different for each stage of the model, depending on the circumstances of the market environment or the morale of the staff in question.

No list of techniques could ever be completely comprehensive, as new ways to tackle old problems are constantly being invented or adapted, but the review of things to consider in Table 3.2 may help you to identify what may be appropriate for your particular performance improvement issue or for your participant group.

ISOLATING THE OBJECTIVES

One obvious starting point is what you hope to achieve by implementing the programme. In other words, decide on your objectives. Formulating a main objective and perhaps a few related subsidiary objectives is not easy. There are many interwoven business problems to be resolved during any given period. Like a doctor, you need to separate the symptoms from the disease. If the human audit is sufficiently rigorous, you should be able to identify specific aims for specific groups.

Within a sales organization, objectives come with the territory.

TYPICAL SALES TEAM OBJECTIVES

- Increase sales overall.
- Increase sales of specific products.
- Increase sales to particular clients.
- Increase sales through particular distribution systems.
- Increase sales in specific local regions.
- Increase sales of additional/complementary services.
- Introduce new products/services.
- Improve client retention.
- Improve repeat orders/new orders.
- Improve the level of average sales (quality).
- Run out old stock.
- Respond to competitor activity.
- Increase market share.

- Improve call rates and prospecting activity.
- Improve administration/paperwork.
- Improve sales force retention.
- Improve team morale.
- Recruit new sales people.
- Test product knowledge.

Almost all of these sales team objectives can combine with other objectives to a greater or lesser degree. Secondary objectives should not conflict with the main goal. For example, the introduction of a new product or service through a new distribution system should not coincide with a general drive on existing client retention or repeat orders.

In keeping with the principle of 'goal salience', it is likely that the main objective will be more achievable if complementary secondary goals are promoted alongside it. So testing new product knowledge and incentivizing a new product go hand in hand.

Training

The importance of skills training cannot be over-emphasized in the quest to achieve lasting improvement. Incentives by themselves only produce short-term benefits. During the human audit process, training and skills development needs will be uncovered. Such issues need to be tackled if a long-term change is required. But it is not simply a question of booking people on a course or sending out a written briefing.

Oldsmobile

The Oldsmobile Motor Division of General Motors was able to accelerate its ambition for higher customer satisfaction by personalizing a skills development programme to each individual dealership. The process involved dealership employees completing a customer satisfaction survey from their customers' perspective.

The results were then compared with the most recent customer satisfaction survey for that dealership.

The gaps provided the basis for three interactive customer satisfaction training modules over the following nine months. Success in the modules enabled the dealership to earn back part of the initial enrolment fee. All 65 of the original pilot dealerships increased their Customer Satisfaction Index. The system was then rolled out to the other 2,900 dealers.

Financial services compliance issues

A major UK financial services organization was under pressure from the industry regulators to become better at identifying customer needs before proposing financial solutions. Legislation was introduced to ensure that sales people were trained to an appropriate standard, and licences were issued to competent practitioners. Those who failed were taken out of the market and retrained accordingly. However the organization was still receiving far too many customer 'factfinds' which were inaccurate or simply not completed correctly. If the trend was left unchecked the company could find itself facing a substantial fine and perhaps a forced withdrawal from the market.

An incentive scheme was devised to reward 'compliance' with a specific number of fields of data which were deemed to be mandatory by the industry regulators. If the factfind was sent into the administration centre with errors, it would be returned to the sales person for correction and no commission would be paid on that customer's file until the errors were rectified. Sales people were rewarded with retail vouchers for every compliant factfind. In addition those sales people who achieved the highest proportion of error-free completed factfinds were invited to a country house with their partner for a hosted weekend of recognition. Within three months 95 per cent of factfinds were submitted error-free and the process problem was solved once and for all, simply by focusing attention on the problem with sufficient communication and incentives to make it an issue for sales people.

Measuring non-sales staff

Beyond the sales team arena, businesses often experience problems in defining measurable objectives, particularly if administration or line staff have never been measured before, except during formal appraisals. But non-sales people can be given objectives. The big debate is whether the cost of setting up and monitoring staff performance is worth the investment. In some cases it may not be.

TYPICAL STAFF OBJECTIVES

- Reduce absenteeism.
- Reduce costs.
- Invite ideas for higher efficiency.
- Promote teamwork and loyalty.
- Promote inter-departmental cooperation.
- Improve safety.
- Improve timekeeping.
- Increase productivity.
- Better staff retention.
- Improve quality of telephone skills.
- Improve general communication skills.
- Monitor project progress.
- Check on morale.
- Check on training effectiveness.
- Improve budgetary control.
- Referral of sales opportunities.
- Recruitment of new staff.
- Direct sales (if applicable).

With enough will to involve everyone in the organization in performance improvement, much can be achieved. But deciding the objectives is not enough. They must be measurable and have specific numbers attached to them, otherwise they become nothing more substantial than a wish list.

QUANTITATIVE OBJECTIVES

To increase sales to clients by 20 per cent, by introducing new product Y and increasing orders retained by 5 per cent.

The quantitative figure that is set needs to meet the criteria of reality. Has such a figure ever been achieved before? If not, what is so different about the new circumstances (apart from general optimism) to suggest you can achieve it this time? Are there any external factors in the marketplace such as legislation or the economy which might skew your quantifiable objective, either now or during the campaign? Will participants find the figure challenging but achievable? Or will they think you are just being far too hopeful? In a changing market where only you have access to positive trend research, but the general current mood is cautious, you need to share that research with participants so they can adjust their personal assessment of the future and change their behaviour accordingly.

For non-sales participants or support staff you can still quantify a remarkable number of so-called 'soft' tasks: the speed at which administration is completed; the quality of telephone contacts with internal and external customers; the reduction of accidents; the usage of stationery, photocopiers and the like; retention of staff. All these issues impinge on performance improvement in a highly measurable way and so can form part of an unequivocal programme in which everyone can take part.

Qualitative objectives can also be measured by surveys of perceived performance improvements. They are no less valid, as often perceptions are the reality when it comes to human behaviour.

In some cases, it may not be possible to allocate the necessary resources to track individual performance. This is particularly true within the multi-integrated activities of large listed companies. Although your ideal measurement may be to record all telephone calls during a programme and analyse their content, the incremental benefit may not be enough to cover the cost of the campaign.

There will be many activities that you can measure, but more is not always better. You need to isolate those performance indicators that have the greatest impact on the bottom line to get the best return on your investment.

Judgement by peers

We were once asked by a multinational IT company to devise a scheme to encourage performance improvement for all staff, including support and administration personnel. They had experienced sales incentives in the past but felt that directing the reward towards the front-line sellers alone did not truly reflect the team approach of a successful IT systems sale. We investigated all aspects of the process of the sale, and discovered that virtually every support department was involved at some stage in the completion of the contract. But the cost of analysing job tasks, setting robust measures and monitoring support staff performance was far too great when compared with the likely incremental profit. The solution? We proposed the idea that the people who can judge your performance best are your peers. So, why not get them to nominate colleagues who are perceived to have done a 'good job' over a given period?

Guidelines were discussed to provide 'voters' with what the company would consider to be good performance, that is, a policy statement of quality service. All nominations would then go forward, countersigned by the manager, to a national league. Those with the highest total number of votes were recognized publicly and rewarded appropriately. All awards were underpinned by a requirement for each department/division to achieve its profit target during the campaign period, otherwise the reward would not be paid out. The programme ran for three years and operated across 12 European countries in several languages.

Quality versus quantity

In many non-sales scenarios there is a trade-off between the cost of tracking individual performance and the incremental benefit.

In the example quoted above, it would certainly have been possible to measure individuals' performance from regular appraisals and devise a reward mechanism which would pay out on specific achievement of key performance indicators, or indeed any range of other process measures the organization may set. However the cost of collecting, collating and communicating that information could well be in excess of any gain for the business. As always, you need to take a view on the value of the exercise compared with the benefit to the business. In the final analysis, it was felt that the less accurate system of voting for peers was more cost-effective than a full individual audit of personal performance, particularly as the programme needed to be run cross-border and across many different cultures.

INCENTIVE TECHNIQUES FOR INDIVIDUAL PARTICIPANTS

Once the objectives have been decided, the next step is to find the right range of incentive techniques to deliver the best chance of a good result. Each element serves a specific purpose, but always check you have not cancelled out one element by introducing a complementary complication. The overriding factor should be to keep it simple. Imagine the participants reading the rules for the first time. Will they understand what is required? Will they understand the measure? Will they be able to plot their progress? Will they be able to change their behaviour? Will it be easy to participate?

1. Leaguing system

The most common mistake made in setting up a motivation programme structure is to base performance on absolute measures: top volume producer, highest team total, top national sales achievement. Every scheme needs winners, but if the winners can all be predicted at the beginning of the programme then you will fail to motivate anyone, beyond those who are already established as 'leading players'. Careful note should be made of what people will perceive as 'fair'. (Whether it is fair or not in reality is another matter.) If everyone is ranked in order of absolute total volume, there will be few surprises at the end of the campaign and very little for those middle-band achievers or new recruits to aim for.

One simple way to create winners at many levels is to 'league' everyone. Within a sales environment this will involve putting similarly achieving sales units together in a discrete league where they can compete with each other for the top awards.

Simple leaguing example

Problem: 100 dealerships, between £5 million and £100 million turnover.

Solution: Create three equal leagues based on current turnover, with awards for the top two in each league. Six winners can be produced, therefore everyone has about a one in 17 chance of winning rather than no chance at all below, say, the 30th ranked dealership.

League 1	League 2	League 3
Dealer A	Dealer D	Dealer G
Dealer B	Dealer E	Dealer H
Dealer C	Dealer F	Dealer I
"	"	"
"	"	"

With this type of structure any participant can calculate that his or her chances of being a winner are higher than if he or she simply has to be in the top turnover group. With this system even a modestly performing dealer could qualify.

One objection to this system may be that you are rewarding too many lower-turnover dealers. You can tweak the structure according to your objectives by creating differing numbers of qualifiers per turnover league.

More complex leaguing example

League 1	League 2	League 3
Dealer A	Dealer D	Dealer I
Dealer B	Dealer E	Dealer J
Dealer C	Dealer F	Dealer K
	Dealer G	Dealer L
	Dealer H	Dealer M
		Dealer N
		Dealer O
		Dealer P

In this way you can skew the chances of winning to those who produce habitually larger levels of turnover. This structure satisfies the large dealers, who have a better chance (in their own perception) of being top. It also helps to encourage the smaller dealers, as they no longer have to compete like for like with the larger dealers.

However, the middle band in any group of competitors often has the biggest capacity to improve (those ranked between 30th and 70th in a group of 100), so you may be wiser to consider how much more overall 'performance' you could get by giving the middle band the best chance of winning. For example, you need to do your sums, but it is likely that a 10 per cent overall increase from league 2 would be worth more on the bottom line than a similar level of achievement from leagues 1 and 3, because there are so many more middle-band performers than other performers.

You do not necessarily need to publish how many competitors there are in each league to everyone in all leagues, if you think those with a lower chance of winning will feel discriminated against. As long as you tell those in any particular league how many places there are in their league, that is usually all they are interested in.

Within a staff environment, leaguing could be done by employee grade, job function or size of business unit. You may need to consider more creative criteria for placing people or groups of people in similar leagues. It could be number of transactions processed, the size of the local catchment area, rural or inner city, old or modern plant or equipment. Although the measures for staff usually need much more research and consideration to provide adequate checks and balances, making a staff scheme fair can be achieved with a little ingenuity.

2.   Close-ended and open-ended

Structural choices often revolve around whether the competition should be open-ended or close-ended. In essence this means the difference between rewarding winners who achieve a personal target, regardless of other competitors' performance, or having a specific number of winners, regardless of the individual's performance.

Close-ended schemes usually rank performance from top to bottom and offer, say, the top 10 per cent the 'big prize'. With 100 participants there would be 10 winners, the top 10 only. This type of system is favoured where the company does not want to take the risk of over-achievement and having to provide expensive per-head awards on the basis of freak market conditions or some unexpected loophole in the rules. In essence it is a defensive tactic from a diffident sponsor, who may long ago in the motivational history of the company have got its fingers burnt. It is less effective than an open-ended scheme, but at least you have a fixed budget. (See Table 3.3.)

Open-ended schemes are much more effective. People compete against their own target or a predetermined performance standard, and feel more committed to a target which matches their situation. If they over-achieve, so much the better. Additional enhancements of the reward can be built in to encourage continuing improvement during the campaign period, once the target is reached. (See Table 3.4.)

Some careful analysis needs to be carried out prior to launch to agree a threshold that will be meaningful but challenging. In practice you might predetermine that you wished to reward 20 per cent of the participant universe. You would look up last year's

Table 3.3 The advantages and disadvantages of close-ended schemes

Advantages	Disadvantages
● Known budget ● Specific number of winners ● Rewards established participants ● Easy to monitor/report ● Top participants keep performing right up to the end of the campaign, if they are within the winning echelon	● Suggests company has a budget problem, ie does not want everyone to be a winner ● Only motivates top echelon ● Novices/middle band cannot win ● Tends not to reward improvement ● Winners can be predicted within a short space of time

performance statistics and choose a threshold that will deliver rewards to all those in the top 20 per cent. You could argue that this is no different to setting up a close-ended scheme. The difference is that participants perceive the threshold to be a personal goal to aim for, which they can plan to achieve. You cannot do anything about the performance of others in a closed scheme other than hope they fail. At least a specific threshold is an objective the participant can aim for without reference to other people. Competing with yourself is a powerful motivator.

There are many variations of open-ended and close-ended programmes to suit most requirements in any market situation. Work through the cost implications of various outcomes and test some likely result scenarios. There is always the risk that your structure may reward the wrong people for the wrong type of performance, so it is vital to 'walk through' the process to see the reward cost liability of not achieving the objectives.

3. Commit-to-win (sometimes called 'bid and make')

Participants declare in advance what performance increase (percentage improvement, specific threshold, number of tasks

Table 3.4 The advantages and disadvantages of open-ended schemes

Advantages	Disadvantages
● Participants compete against personal targets ● Everyone feels they can win ● Different targets can be set for different people in the same scheme ● Scheme perceived as more equitable	● Cost not known until end of campaign ● No single target suits everyone ● Unusual market conditions can create too many/too few winners

accomplished) they will attain. The higher they aim, the higher the reward if successful. If they aim low and achieve high, the rewards are less than if they had pitched high in the first place. The objective is to get sophisticated participants to bet against their own performance and aim higher than average. Experience shows that in overall terms more people achieve higher performance levels than they would otherwise do if given a set threshold. People are often surprised how much they can improve, given the right conditions. However, this option requires a certain amount of knowledge about personal past performance so that they can set challenging levels of future performance. Such a structure is unlikely to work if the participants are competing for the first time, or are working with new performance standards or a new market situation.

A recent sophistication of this concept is to allow participants to bid for rewards with their accumulated points as if in an auction. Online software similar to ebay has now made it possible to make redeeming the reward a fun activity, not just an administrative task.

4. Escalator

Points are awarded for achieving the threshold, with higher levels of points as each level is passed above that threshold.

Table 3.5 An escalator example

Level	Payment
Threshold	1,000
110%	2,000
120%	4,000
130%	8,000

Setting the points levels depends on being able to predict from past performance how many participants are likely to reach the upper levels. If you are thoroughly confident, you may decide to 'escalate' *ad infinitum,* but most people set a cut-off level beyond which the rewards are fixed, or you risk being hostage to freak market conditions and bankrupting the company. (See Table 3.5.)

5. All or nothing

For those who like a challenge (and like to justify every penny to the financial department) one approach is to award nothing unless the threshold is achieved. Once it is, all performance points are retrospective. This enables you to set a challenging target (such as budget plus 20 per cent), but promise a big reward in return. It has the major selling point of being simple to understand, but it does have one drawback. With no lower-level rewards, average performers tend to believe that they cannot achieve the target and hence do not commit themselves as enthusiastically as you would like. Clearly, you need to have an understanding board if your team over-achieves against your expectations and you have a fixed budget. It is often the case that performance improvement funds are not flexible – they are usually part of a promotional budget based on sales or market share. With variations like 'all or nothing' you can end up paying substantial rewards which will eat into other promotional areas if the programme is not carefully set up.

6. Sweepstake/lottery/raffle

The most unsatisfactory variation, but quite widespread in practice, is the sweepstake approach. Each percentage improvement or sale is worth one ticket in the 'reward sweepstake'. The more you improve or sell, the more chances you have of winning. This type of structure is mostly used by unsophisticated clients with an inadequate budget for the task in hand. By using clever promotion you can make the prize fund look very attractive. Although mathematically the higher achievers stand a better chance of winning the better rewards, it rarely works out like that in practice. More often a mediocre performer carries away the big prize by pure chance and feels embarrassed, while the higher-level performers feel cheated and the sponsor (client company) is surprised it has left such a nasty taste. A refinement could be to restrict the 'chance' element to those who have attained a specific level, such as 120 per cent, thereby ensuring higher-level performers will win the higher-level prizes. There could be differing values of awards depending on the threshold participants cross.

Promotional variations include scratchcards, sealed envelopes, lucky squares, lucky number phone-ins, matching cards, every fifth sale and a whole host of other devices to make the prize a secret until all is revealed. But it is still all based on chance and this is never a wholly satisfactory way to incentivize or reward performance improvement.

7. Fast starts, fast finishes

One of the problems with introducing any corporate initiative is the speed at which staff take up the challenge. The take-up is normally very slow for a variety of reasons – inadequate launch communication, misunderstanding of the rules, too busy functionally to react quickly, an attitude of 'not invented here so I will not cooperate'.

One way to improve things is to build in an artificial accelerator at the beginning of the programme, normally known as a 'fast start'. This could involve extra credits in the opening period of the campaign to focus attention on getting the campaign introduced quickly and establishing the ground rules. An alternative could be to trade early achievement against a specific reduction in the end campaign target, thereby encouraging early performance.

This is particularly suitable for new product introductions, where speed of market penetration is essential.

Equally, the final period in any campaign may have specific significance for your market, but most well-constructed schemes do not have a 'fast finish' built in as the incentive itself is to achieve the standard before the end of the period. More typically a fast finish is introduced as an emergency measure to raise the profile of a mediocre campaign or to create more winners than would be expected, say, in a recessional period or following the unforeseen withdrawal of a specific product during the campaign which was beyond your control. (Double credits in the final month is a popular device.)

8. Weighting performance

One of the key principles in structuring a campaign is to achieve the participants' perception that the competitive element is fair. In other words, they all feel they can earn something at one level or another. To achieve the perception of 'fairness', you need to consider a series of checks and balances so that participants do not immediately assess their chances of being successful as nil. So, for distributors with differing turnover, you might adopt a league approach (see above). For staff in a sparsely populated area you may have to weight their volume of administration against a busier city area so that comparisons are fair.

In some industries you may wish to remove certain products from the campaign, such as those that tend to sell at predictable levels anyway, or those that are not available on a national basis. Or you may wish to give 'customer service' twice as many credits as attendance, to emphasize its relative importance.

You may decide that you want to measure people by the amount of the improvement rather than the volume of activity. Measuring improvement against a personal benchmark is another way to equalize performance so that all participants feel they have an equal chance of success.

VARIATIONS FOR TEAM PARTICIPANTS

The variations in structure can be applied to teams as if they were individuals, except for one thing, namely peer group pressure. People working together exact considerable pressure on each other when they are aiming for a common objective. Depending on the degree of focus and leadership, the result can be better or worse than for the same people competing as individuals. You need to decide what best fits your corporate objectives.

- **Total team performance.** The team competes as if it were an individual and the rewards are equally distributed among the team, regardless of input, grade or experience.
- **Points pool.** The team competes in the normal way, but the reward is divided up according to the measurable contribution of each individual. This is relatively easy to define within a sales environment and less so for administrative staff, but it does depend on the scheme. If staff are being objectively measured on such standards as absenteeism, timekeeping, attendance at training sessions, product knowledge and procedural accuracy, it is quite possible to reward according to individual performance as well as rewarding the whole team.
- **Personal bonus.** The team could achieve a group standard for a specific team reward, with certain individuals receiving additional rewards for individual performance.
- **Rank order.** Individuals within a team are rewarded in rank order of their individual performance.

Although throughout this book it has been argued that everyone in any job can be measured, the costs for measuring some types of employee can outweigh any incremental benefit, so rewarding the team may be best. However, it is even more important to ensure that the group task is clearly understood and that the challenge being set is perceived as fair. There will always be individuals who feel that they are unfairly targeted or that their local circumstances do not allow them to perform well. If this is the consensus view of a team, the value of the motivation scheme will be negative rather than positive. Individuals can be talked round to a positive view. Negative teams are hard work, and you

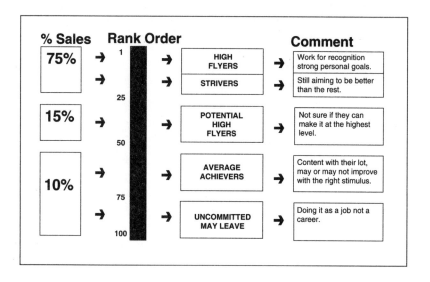

Figure 3.4 The middle-band concept

may find it less destructive to allow them to opt out rather than spread dissent. A vociferous but small number of isolated individuals is easier to handle than a large, disgruntled team.

THE MIDDLE-BAND CONCEPT

A key element in deciding how to structure any incentive campaign is to know who you are trying to influence the most. Taking sales as a measure, it is a well-known phenomenon that a disproportionate amount of your sales comes from the top quartile of your entire distribution chain. In effect sales are skewed to come from a minority of your sales people, so it is right that a lot of effort goes into encouraging those at the top to do more. However, in overall terms, a 10 per cent increase in sales from the very top echelon is actually less than a 10 per cent increase from those who sit in the middle-band, say from the bottom of the second quartile to the top of the fourth quartile. (See Figure 3.4.)

One strategy to take advantage of this phenomenon is to offer enhanced recognition for the high-flyers but actually spend more

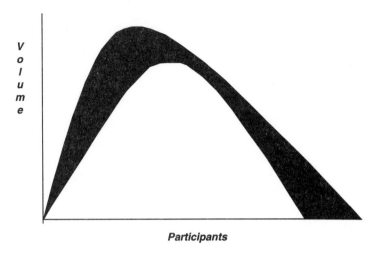

Figure 3.5 Sales distribution graph after an incentive

on the middle-level rewards so that the programme reaches down into the second and third quartiles, thereby encouraging more overall sales.

An easy way to explain the concept to your sponsor is to construct a distribution graph to show the number of participants who currently contribute the most sales (or whatever the financial measure is). On the left-hand side there is a sharp climb in the number of sales people achieving up to the average level of sales. Once the average is reached it falls off very slowly, revealing a long tail of higher performers. The idea of an incentive scheme is to move the whole area under the curve to the right, creating a shorter initial climb (and therefore more participants) to the new improved average, and a higher number of high achievers in the tail beyond the average. The area between the two curves could be deemed to be the incremental gain as a result of the incentive. (See Figure 3.5.)

HOW LONG SHOULD THE INCENTIVE PROGRAMME LAST?

Some experienced sales directors never run any scheme longer than three months. Some human resources managers would not contemplate a performance improvement scheme which runs for less than a year. The answer lies somewhere in between, and depends on the business objectives. There is no prescriptive answer for every situation, but experience suggests a few pointers.

- **Standards programmes.** Where you are hoping to change working practices over the long term you will need to build in time for a pilot test and working roll-out. Invariably business cycles need a year to work themselves through, so a general view would be an 18-month period, comprising three months pilot, three months assessment and amendments, and 12 months initial programme.
- **Tactical sales campaigns.** The length of tactical schemes is usually dictated by the call cycle of the industry or the length of the selling season. Anywhere between six weeks and three months is normal. A programme that lasts four weeks or less will rely heavily on very good launch communications within the network, as even simple incentives take at least a week to get round even a modest-size distribution chain. With a short campaign period it is difficult to influence any change of behaviour before the programme ends.
- **Annual programmes.** Where business is relatively predictable and not subject to fashion or consumer switching, annual programmes are more normal, tied into the financial reporting year. The structure could involve two or three tactical campaigns to coincide with known business peaks, and an overlaid scheme running for 12 months to incentivize and reward consistently higher-level performance over the year.

  Although the marketing department may be aware when the tactical schemes will run, the participants will not, ensuring the company takes advantage of the element of surprise.

  Within financial services a typical incentive programme might look like that shown in Table 3.6.

  Within the automotive industry an alternative approach may be necessary to respond to market blips, combining car sales and aftersales (service, accessories). See Table 3.7.

Table 3.6 Annual programme – tactical and strategic

Month		
Jan		
Feb		F
March		u
April	Tactical	l
May	Tactical	l
June	Tactical	
July		Y
Aug		e
Sept	Tactical	a
Oct	Tactical	r
Nov		
Dec		

{ In this case we have a three-month tactical campaign in the spring and a two-month campaign in early autumn, with an overlaid scheme for consistent performance running January to December

Table 3.7 A typical incentive programme for the car industry

Month	Cars	Aftersales
Jan	Tactical	Tactical
Feb	Tactical	Tactical
March	Tactical	
April		
May		
June		Tactical
July	Tactical	Tactical
Aug	Tactical	Tactical
Sept	Tactical	
Oct		
Nov		Tactical
Dec		Tactical

{ To incentivize showroom sales a first-quarter campaign and a summer campaign may be appropriate. But this would be supported by a parallel scheme of tactical aftersales incentives to capture market share during the 'distress' winter period and the mid-year 'days out with the family' period.

- **Riding the peaks.** People often debate whether tactical incentives should run during peaks or troughs in the revenue cycle. There is a natural reluctance to distribute rewards for sales that will largely happen anyway. Surely, we should be targeting the troughs to improve our spread and iron out the dips?

Each market is different but the most cost-effective schemes reap the most incremental performance when they are run during average months running into a peak or from a peak to an average period. Schemes run during troughs provide only a modest improvement and often prove to be an expensive way to buck the market. The explanation is logical. The reason for the trough is usually an unchanging market characteristic (ice cream sells poorly in winter) which no amount of promotion will change. The principle is to boost sales in a favourable environment and try to prolong that peak as much as possible, or until such time as the incremental returns are less than the investment.

RULES AND REGULATIONS

Whether it is for staff or sales people, the rules and regulations of any performance-improvement programme need careful thought for a variety of reasons:

- Participants need to feel the way their performance will be judged is fair.
- Participants need to know what will be included in terms of performance measures.
- Participants need to know what the rewards will be.
- Participants need to know about any hidden catches (tax liabilities, no alternatives to the stated awards).
- The company needs to communicate clear parameters.
- The company may need to exclude certain elements of performance.
- The company may need to protect itself against deliberate misinterpretation by participants to gain additional rewards.
- The company needs a written record of what is promised against specific criteria so that it can estimate its financial investment and liability.

If the rules are written by the finance director, it is likely you will never launch the programme, because there will always be some loophole, however unlikely, that cannot be closed by terms and conditions. The important thing is to keep the drafting of the rules in perspective and produce something that clearly states the way the programme works, while protecting the company against inadvertent or mischievous misinterpretation.

For most campaigns, the rules need to follow these guidelines:

- Who can participate?
- What do participants have to do?
- Duration?
- What rewards, at what level?
- Clarify any liabilities (tax, personal cost of travel to event)?
- Arbitrator in case of dispute?
- Communication policy during the campaign and at the end?

With complex programmes, which may have four or five variants for different participant grades or types (sales, administration, plant, branches, distribution), you may need to produce a broad set of general rules for the glossy brochure and issue more detailed rules for each subgroup of participants, depending on their involvement. But the golden rule is to ensure each participant has a copy of the rules relevant to his or her grade. Many companies make the mistake of only supplying the group manager with the rules. However adept a communicator that manager may be, he or she is unlikely to cover all the angles, resulting in some participants working to a performance standard that could actually have been excluded from the campaign. Full disclosure is the key.

Rules example

Here is an example of the rules for a fictitious distributors' incentive:

1. The 'Go for Gold' sales incentive campaign will run from Monday 2 January to Friday 31 March at the close of the normal business day.
2. All registered distributors may take part, except for those who are not yet accredited. Any distributors receiving accreditation during the campaign period may only participate at the discretion of the regional director.

3. Distributors will be measured against their previously agreed campaign target for conquest sales only. No credit will be given for repeat sales or any service sales.
4. Distributors who achieve 50 per cent or more of their campaign target by the end of the first month of the campaign will receive the 'fast-start' award, as described in the launch brochure/website.
5. Distributors who achieve one of the three top places in their league by the end of the campaign will be invited to an event to be hosted by the company in Paris for three nights in May. Winners will be expected to cover their own costs to and from the point of departure.
6. Distributors will receive a monthly update on the website of their performance. Those without internet access can request a faxed update from the sales operations department.
7. Winners will be notified at the end of the first month for the fast-start awards and at the end of the third month for the Paris award by letter from the relevant regional director, subject to a final audit of the claimed sales.
8. The awards are discretionary and no cash alternatives will be offered in any circumstances.
9. All awards are taxable in the hands of the recipients and it is the duty of winners to declare the reward as a benefit in kind when reporting end of year tax calculations to the tax authorities.
10. Any disputes will be decided by the sales director whose decision is final.
11. The company reserves the right to alter or cancel the programme in the light of adverse trading conditions or circumstances beyond its control.

Although the language used is quite formal, the rules set out very clearly what the participants have to do and when the awards will be made. It is important to clarify the policy on taking cash alternatives and the situation regarding tax so that there is no possibility of misunderstanding at a later date. If you know of a specific loophole that has been exploited in the past by participants, you can use the rules to close it once and for all.

TIERED REWARD SYSTEMS

Few effective campaigns rely on only one single type of reward item. The more common approach is to tier the rewards according to the expected levels of achievement or the likely participants. Typically the top achievers may qualify for a group or hosted travel event, the next group down may qualify for retail vouchers or merchandize items and the lowest group may receive a specific item of recognition. In more sophisticated companies the group travel event itself may comprise two or more levels of qualification, perhaps taking higher-level achievers to a long-haul destination and the second-level achievers to a less exotic place. Or the second tier might stay for only four days, while the top tier stay for seven days.

The same creativity can also apply to lower-level rewards. You may decide to set a lower threshold that participants need to achieve before they are admitted to the higher rewards. You may decide that the very highest achievers could be enrolled into an 'honours' club with various levels of entry and reward, either over a short period, or more usually over a full financial year. The main advantage of the tiered approach is the ability to stretch the rewards down into the middle of the participant database. The per head costs of group travel, especially if you include a 'significant other' in the incentive, can be quite expensive. You can make the budget go further by reducing the number of top-level travel rewards and increasing the number of vouchers or merchandise rewards, thereby increasing the total number of winners.

In terms of appealing to as many sections of your participant database as possible, you need to consider tiered rewards, because whatever reward you choose there will always be a significant minority for whom that particular offer does not work. Being flexible with your rewards is the key to a good campaign structure.

SUMMARY

- Learn from the history of motivation theory.
- Apply the 10 motivation theory principles, but only when appropriate.
- Isolate your objectives.
- Set quantifiable aims.
- Use appropriate incentive techniques.
- 'Walk through' the likely outcome.
- Check the rules for comprehensibility.
- Consider tiered reward systems.

4

Building the
budget

I wouldn't invest in a business that didn't invest in its people.
Sir John Harvey-Jones

Once you have established who is to be included and which programme structure to use, the next step is to propose a suitable
budget. As large numbers of people are likely to be involved in
the improvement process, any expenditure will be significant. A
budget for motivation should be seen as a medium-term investment with a specific pay-back period. In most cases the budget
will be self-liquidating, though proving this to be the case
depends on what measurement standards were introduced at the
outset to determine the incremental gain on the original investment. The only decision will be whether the company can afford
to risk the initial set-up costs, because if a programme does not
work, for whatever reason, the scheme will not produce any
reward costs.

Setting a budget for a performance improvement programme
is no different from setting any other budget for future expenditure. Certain assumptions need to be taken into account.
However, many organizations insist that incentive or performance programmes need to be 'self-funding' and seen to be so.

The fact that the entire company is not self-funding until the report and accounts are filed at the end of the financial year is another issue.

No one can guarantee the future success of a performance improvement campaign. If they could, solutions could be logged and filed with a firm of reputable management consultants, and trotted out when the right conditions prevail. But there are ways to minimize the risk of failure. Many of these are described in this book. One way is to draft a sensible budget and make some reasoned, rather than simply hopeful, predictions of success.

THE CONCEPT OF INCREMENTAL PROFIT

Before you begin to add up all the expected costs, you should examine the overall objective: incremental profit. All other things being equal, a well-planned sales incentive programme should produce additional turnover of between 10 and 20 per cent, sometimes more. Depending on your general view of the business climate, you can draw up an incremental profit objective.

Incremental profit example

Within the campaign period chosen, company A obtains £1 million revenue from the sale of its product. An incentive scheme is suggested to capitalize on and lengthen an already successful period.

1. At 20 per cent additional sales, the campaign would provide £1.2 million in revenue.
2. You know that additional revenue earns profits at 35 per cent margin (so this will bring in £70,000 extra profit).
3. The company works on an allowance of 33.3 per cent to generate new business, so £23,310 will be available in the form of promotion and rewards.
4. If the fixed costs of launch and promotion are deemed to be an already budgeted marketing cost, the actual money available for rewards would be £23,310.

The higher the margin – and it may be much higher if production set-up costs are ignored – the higher the amount available for rewards.

Summary

- Expected revenue without incentive, £1 million.
- Expected revenue with incentive, £1.2 million.
- Incremental revenue, £200,000.
- Profit margin at 35 per cent = £70,000.
- Incentive budget at 33.3 per cent of profit margin = £23,310.

Setting the campaign target

The incentive budget of £23,310 represents about 11.7 per cent (to be precise, 11.655 per cent) of additional sales. It would therefore be reasonable to suggest a campaign target of budget plus 12 per cent (£1.12 million). So, when the target is achieved, £23,310 will become retrospectively available for rewards and therefore the campaign becomes self-funding. But, once turnover exceeds target, you can afford to be more generous with the rewards (see Table 4.1).

Provided the campaign target covers the original budget and the marginal cost of the rewards, a sales incentive can be self-funding.

COST HEADINGS

Once you have determined the incremental profit and therefore the campaign target, you need to consider what costs you are likely to incur. They will be either fixed or variable.

Fixed costs

- initial roughs, research;
- creative concept fees;
- design for literature, images;
- design for web site;

Table 4.1 Campaign reward scenarios

Budget £1 million	Target £1,120,000
1. 90% of target achieved (*£1,008,000 turnover*)	• No rewards because target was not achieved • As the budget was achieved, plus £8,000, set-up costs could be amortized
2. 100% of target achieved (*£1,120,000 turnover*)	• Rewards paid out at 33.3% of additional turnover; £40,000 • At 35% promotional margin, the company pockets £42,000 in incremental sales
3. 110% of target achieved (*£1,232,000 turnover*)	• Rewards paid out at 33.3% of additional turnover; £77,256 • At 35% promotional margin, the company pockets £81,200 in incremental sales
4. 120% of target achieved (*£1,344,000 turnover*)	• Rewards paid out at 33.3% of additional turnover; £114,552 • At 35% promotional margin, the company pockets £120,400 in incremental sales

- artwork;
- copywriting;
- video scripting;
- video production;
- video copies, plus packaging;
- printed materials, web pages;
- collation, packaging;
- computer system set-up, new software;
- distribution, launch postage;
- training manuals.

It is difficult to be precise about costs, as much depends on the nature of the tasks to be completed. But in the unlikely event that the campaign has no effect whatsoever on performance, the initial fixed costs of between 10 and 12 per cent will not be recouped.

Variable administration costs

- computer system, administration;
- bulletin stationery;
- distribution of bulletins, other communications;
- reward-based handling fees;
- selective training costs;
- agency consultancy, if applicable (10–15 per cent);
- mid-campaign research;
- end-campaign research.

Sometimes a 'win fee' may be appropriate. In other words, instead of the agency charging a set percentage of the expenditure as their fee, it might be so confident of success that it reduces its overall percentage in favour of a contingency payment based on the success of the programme. There is clearly a risk here for the agency as it needs to be very sure that the client's organization will deliver the expected improvements in order for it to claim the fee. Win fees are more likely with a large budget where the client is attempting to minimize the downside with a structure or idea that it is perhaps not confident with. Be very careful though in agreeing the criteria for awarding the win fee. You could end up paying a lot more than a standard fee if the economy is doing well and other market factors beyond the control of the incentives agency lead to increased performance.

Variable reward costs

This leaves an amount of between 73 and 80 per cent of the budget to cover reward and taxes. In the United Kingdom, assuming a current grossed-up payment of 25 per cent for basic-rate tax

Table 4.2   Budget summary based on £100,000

1.	Set-up and launch	£12,000
2.	Ongoing administration and fees	£18,000
3.	Rewards	£55,000
4.	Tax grossed up at 28%	£15,400
		£100,400

paid awards, the actual reward element comes to approximately 55 per cent of the total budget.

From this example, particularly if tax is to be included, the sponsor needs to be aware that just over half the original budget will be set aside for rewards. With a sales force of say 500, the initial calculation of 'What's in it for them?' on a per head basis of £200 has been whittled down to just £110 per head.

Clearly some savings can be made, but each budget heading is there to serve a particular function. By diluting any element, you may be diluting the impact of the entire programme, and this will lead to fewer incremental sales and a hefty bill for set-up costs.

External set-up and handling fees paid to agencies are always negotiable, but you need to bear in mind that the lower the fees, the more likely it is that the agency will not be able to sustain as much account-handling time as should be necessary, risking poor administration of the programme. Quality of administration is always worth paying for, whenever you are purchasing marketing services externally.

Terms and procurement

In recent years many organizations have been considering ways to reduce costs by outsourcing marketing services to a small roster of chosen suppliers that meet specific criteria. This has been commonplace within the advertising industry but less so in so-called below-the-line agencies. All that has changed. Incentive agencies and performance improvement consultancies are now being considered in a similar way, as 'strategic suppliers' within certain industry sectors, with interesting consequences.

Procurement departments in major organizations have acquired the skills to be able to make value judgements between competing incentive agencies, and have been able to specify very clearly what is required in staff hours and bought-in services to fulfil a brief. This has had the effect of reducing fees and to some extent polarizing the market into agencies that are big enough to work on smaller margins and agencies that cannot afford to work with procurement-driven organizations.

Larger agencies have had to develop sophisticated terms and conditions in order to defend themselves against non-payment of fees due from large companies. In former times most motivation programme proposals were presented directly to the marketing or human resources user, who decided which supplier to use. There was no need for smaller agencies to have detailed terms or even an official contract, as in English Law behaviour largely determines whether there is a contract for services. Now that tendering for external services has become more transparent and involves many more people in the sponsoring organization, even small agencies have detailed terms and conditions to ensure their remuneration is protected. So an unforeseen consequence of more procurement has been better protection for small agencies, legally speaking, and the need for even occasional users of incentive agencies to read the small print carefully before committing their organization to an outsourced scheme.

Here is a list of typical headings which may form part of the standard terms and conditions when a buyer purchases incentive or performance improvement services from an external supplier:

- fees;
- expenses;
- client amendments;
- terms of payment;
- purchase tax;
- cancellation, suspension;
- use of materials, copyright;
- warranties, liabilities;
- legality of promotion;
- *force majeure*;
- waiver;
- non-assignment;
- confidentiality;
- notices, legal jurisdiction;
- exchange rates;
- disputes procedure.

As with all legal documents it may not be appropriate to spend expensive legal fees to challenge each and every clause that a supplier proposes. You could end up spending more on legal fees than your total incentives budget. But it is wise to get your in-house legal team to take a view about some specific clauses if you think they are too heavily weighted in favour of the service supplier. The most likely area for disagreement is the section dealing with terms of payment, so you need to be sure that both parties are happy with how the transaction is going to be completed before commencing the programme, particularly if part of the service involves booking hotel rooms or arranging travel services some time in advance.

A word about agencies

Although formal non-cash incentive schemes and performance improvement programmes have been a feature of US business life for half a century, the concept of the 'full-service motivation agency' is a relatively recent idea in Europe. P&MM, the UK agency, conducted several surveys in recent years into buyer behaviour and established that over 70 per cent of performance improvement programmes were undertaken by client companies, with many organizations claiming no knowledge of specialist agencies in this field of marketing services. In fact most clients would turn to their advertising agency or sales promotion agency, before approaching a motivation or incentive agency. They would then front up any programme suggestion, and subcontract the analysis and reward fulfilment to a variety of below-the-line specialist suppliers.

The good news is that there are now a number of incentive and performance improvement specialists who operate ethical and reliable companies with enough clients to offer informed advice. But, as with most areas of marketing services, it is worthwhile looking into the historical roots of the agency you appoint, as those roots may well dictate the type of advice you are given.

Whatever the commercial title of the agency, most come from one of the six following product or service backgrounds:

- merchandise;
- travel;

- sales promotion;
- training;
- event management;
- conference production.

Some have successfully integrated all their products into a completely rounded service, adding consultancy to create bespoke solutions for performance improvement problems. Others have yet to leave their product roots behind, and enjoy variable levels of success, depending on the brief.

As the Marquis de la Grange said back in 1872, 'When we ask advice, we are usually looking for an accomplice.' Make sure your chosen agency has the strength in depth to give objective overall advice before investing the entire budget in the agency's favourite product or service.

If things change, so should the budget

Business has a habit of not coming in when you expect it, or in the mix you prefer. With long-term programmes there are many external influences which can affect the eventual cost of an incentive scheme. If you spend too much proportionally on the initial launch, and government legislation or a competitor makes your product obsolete, those fixed costs will be wasted. If you allocate too much credit to a particular product and freak marketing conditions make it the hottest thing since the invention of the frisbee, you may find yourself paying out thousands of pounds in reward to each individual rather than hundreds. If your company merges with, or is bought by, another company, assumptions of who will sell what over a given period will now be somewhat different.

As long as you have set up targets based on incremental sales, the more the merrier. If not, you may have to go cap in hand back to the finance department, which may tell you 'there is no more money', even though you can prove that more sales means more profit. An incremental budget for a subsidiary has a habit of becoming a fixed budget when the parent company has to approve the overspend.

Budgeting guidelines

The most important aspect of any performance improvement scheme is that it should work, and that experiences are built up over the years to do better programmes in the future. Budgeting is all very well but it's what happens in the real world that counts. So do not spend too long calculating and recalculating all the what-ifs. Nevertheless, here are a few guidelines to consider when analysing a budget that might have been produced by an external supplier:

- What is the proportion of fees to the overall expenditure? This should not be more than 20 per cent and should be somewhat less if the supplier is a good trade buyer on your behalf.
- What is the proportion of reward to the overall budget? As we saw above, including the allowance for tax on the benefits provided, it should be a minimum of 55 per cent and may well be more if the programme has been set up correctly.
- Is the fee for administration justified? Often agencies submit a contingency fee for handling the reward and a separate administration fee for regular administrative tasks or for computerization services. The fees will have been calculated on a staff hours basis, so it is perfectly legitimate to ask for the breakdown of staff-hours so you can see if it is reasonable.
- What are the charges for client amendments? Most people are aware that even the best-planned proposals can often bear no relationship to the job that is actually completed. This can have far-reaching consequences when it comes to reconciling the budget at the end of the programme. Get a clear statement of daily charges for client-inspired changes, and make sure your internal sponsors are aware that arbitrary changes of detail will cost more money to implement, so think carefully before you redesign the whole scheme, once the proposal has been accepted by procurement and other internal sponsors.
- What is the cancellation policy for hotels/air tickets proposed as part of the programme? Many performance improvement programmes include some element of travel, domestic or foreign. The proportion of travel spend can be quite high, compared with the costs of administration for example. Often

rooms and flights have to be booked some time in advance of the departure date to secure sufficient facilities for your winning group. However, be aware that third party suppliers have different cancellation clauses depending who they are and where they are, so you need to inform your treasury department what and when you will need to supply advance payments to ensure you have the facilities covered.

The business case

We began this chapter with a discussion about the concept of incremental profit. We tried to determine what additional profits might be generated by an incentive scheme, and therefore what budget would be appropriate to fund that extra profit. At the end of every programme some effort should be made to determine whether the extra profit generated really did pay for the costs of the programme, and therefore what scope there might be to do more programmes in the future. In practice most programmes create many hidden benefits which were unexpected.

For example, the process of registering participants for the programme may have allowed you to create for the first time an accurate list of staff or distributors involved in the sale or marketing process you are attempting to influence. The online magazine that you created to update participants with their performance may become a permanent channel of communication, even though there may be no continuation of the scheme once it is finished. The recognition events and items which were part of the programme may become established in the organizational calendar as 'must-do' activities to maintain morale for future years.

So although budgets are important to get right to establish a sound business case, it should be remembered that incentive schemes are dynamic activities which rely on enthusiastic participation and good communication if they are to be successful. The softer, human outcomes may be just as important as hard figures when it comes to making a final assessment of the overall success of the initiative.

SUMMARY
- The concept of incremental profit means most incentives should be self-funding.
- Campaign targets are different from budgets.
- Examine fixed costs and variable costs in detail.
- When taking external advice beware of being sold inappropriate reward media.
- Recalculate your budget if circumstances change.

5 | Does more money motivate?

The fact that an opinion is widely held is no evidence whatsoever that it is not utterly absurd.

Bertrand Russell

Now that you have identified the business problem, and decided the structure and budget of a performance improvement campaign, there is one ghost to lay before you can begin to consider the reward elements: money. Because offering money is where most people start when it comes to thinking motivationally, we need to examine its efficiency.

Why not just give people more money? It is usually the first reason people give for leaving their current employment. It is the largest expenditure item in any company's overheads. In the developed West, with a long tradition of industrial relations, monetary reward is something everyone can agree about, even if they have differing views about how much.

If in doubt, the pay plan can always be manipulated to suit the type of employee or third party seller. Assuming someone is getting the generally accepted 'going rate' for the job, you can cut the pay cake several different ways:

- basic salary, annual increments;
- commission for each item sold/sales achievement;
- performance-related pay;
- stock options;
- other benefits.

Few companies offer just one of these elements in isolation. A combination of ways to be paid offers the opportunity to reward people on a short-term and a long-term basis, depending on the company's objectives and pay strategy for that particular group of employees.

BASIC SALARY

Provided the job description has been drafted correctly and some soundings have been taken of the local and national market for a particular job role, setting a salary provides the basis for rewarding long-term effort. The advantages to the employer are: its administrative simplicity (the same amount each month), task orientation can be tied directly back to the job description, and differentials in basic pay among the same job grade can reflect loyalty or professional qualifications.

However, as an aid to improving performance, it does very little. There is no incentive to try harder or make any extra effort, beyond the competitive pride or personal job satisfaction of the individual. Deviant behaviour such as absenteeism or deliberate non-cooperation does not usually result in a loss of earnings. Comparison with other employers is easily made, if there are no other incremental benefits within the pay plan, and so there may be difficult and expensive judgements to make at the end of each year at salary review. Because a salary is not usually contingent on job performance, companies that adopt the salary-only approach tend not to establish even basic performance criteria and measurement. This results in a minimum-effort culture where the success of the business rests largely on product development and the economic climate. As Michael Le Boeuf, professor of management, University of New Orleans, points out, 'Reward people for the right behaviour and you get the right results. Fail to reward the right behaviour and you are likely to get the wrong results.'

By not rewarding risk takers, the company rewards precisely the behaviour syndrome it would rather not have. For sales people on a pure salary pay plan, it can lead to missed sales opportunities, loss of top sales employees tempted away by a competitor's bigger salary offer, and the risk that in a cyclic downturn, the company may have far too many sales people for the income they generate.

In practice there are few successful companies that offer just a salary, so it may be more realistic to consider what performance improvement advantages there may be in combining salary with the various forms of performance-related pay.

SALARY PLUS COMMISSION

A basic salary plus a commission for sales people is the most popular way to encourage higher performance improvement. But you have to get the ratio right between salary and commission. If there is too much salary, people tend to perceive the commission as 'fun' money and so it becomes less effective as a driving force. If the commission element is too great, people start to cut corners on quality of service and business ethics to ensure they can at least meet their minimal monthly outgoings.

The general guideline is that anywhere between 15 and 35 per cent represents an effective ratio for commission compared with basic salary, depending on the market sector. However, the commissionable element of any remuneration plan requires sound administration and a thorough understanding of the 'rules of engagement' when deciding what to award. In many industries it is becoming harder and harder to attribute particular sales or contracts to single individuals. Even the archetypal sales person – the life assurance seller – is often supported by technical specialists who assist the sale in complex cases.

For large contract sales, where a relationship has been built up over the years with a succession of representatives, a tender document is normally produced with the assistance of a team of technical staff. It may be the financial director, in the final analysis, who decides what fee to charge, thereby positioning the bid that wins the contract. Should the last sales person in get the commission? Should the support team receive any? Should everyone in the company benefit directly? But perhaps the most difficult aspect of running an effective commission system is defining who made the sale.

DEFINING THE SALE

- Initial desk research into the opportunity (identifying the prospect).
- Initial telephone call.
- Initial letter (not acknowledged).
- Initial letter (acknowledged).
- Voice contact, in person or by phone.
- Credentials presentation.
- Meeting to discuss the specific project.
- Presentation of the response.
- Order taken.

All of these stages in the sale could be deemed to be the crucial moment when the potential client became aware of the potential supplier. But in a mature market where the main players for a particular service or product are known, an incoming contact from the client by letter or telephone could spark off the start of a sales relationship. In such a situation, should the sales person who simply picked up the phone receive commission? If so, should it be the same level of commission as if the sales person had researched the client over two years before finally clinching the deal?

Crediting sales to individuals becomes even more complicated when a company has an existing client bank with many divisions to sell into. Is it still a sale to sell the same thing to the same client two years running? Or, worse still, should commission be paid to a sales person for a sale which is a repeat order when the sales person has not been in contact with the client for two or three years, other than reading reports from the technical team?

If commission levels are minimal, the question of payment is less important, but with levels of 25 to 30 per cent, significant sums are involved which can cause considerable demotivation of support staff, particularly if they know the sales person made no contribution at all to the repeat sale.

Prospecting – rewarding the process

Depending on your business strategy for acquiring new business, you will lend more or less importance to specific prospect-related achievements. You need to find the balance that suits your objectives and culture, and write the rules accordingly. (See Table 5.1.)

Within large corporations that may span several industries, you will need to define whether direct sales made in one division should be credited to a sales person who has a relationship with a totally separate division, but who has no contact with the first division.

A good strategy is to draw up a list of well-defined rules so that there is no doubt about when credit is due, and individual claims do not have to go for adjudication, wasting valuable management time and not furthering the business process in any way. You need to consider all the possible anomalies so that the system is clearly understood by those who are participating and those who are responsible for calculating how much commission is due.

Table 5.1 The prospecting reward process

Activity	Performance improvement strategy
Identifying the prospect	Reward the number of prospects
Initial telephone call	Reward the accuracy of prospect data
Initial letter/follow-up	Reward the ratio of positive responses to letters sent
Voice contact	Reward ratio of calls to prospect voice contact
Credentials	Reward number of credentials made
Briefing meeting	Reward ratio of briefs received to credentials made
Actual sales	Reward ratio of sales to initial telephone call

Commission has been the mainstay for many organizations relying on rapid penetration and distribution within large markets. In some consumer markets where sales depend on aggressive personal marketing (automotive, insurance, high-value home improvements) commission is effective in promoting high-energy levels, fast growth in turnover and wide product distribution. However, the higher the value of the item, the more likely that mis-selling will be subject to legal regulation or trade ethics, resulting in commission disputes, or worse still, deliberate inappropriate selling which tarnishes the entire market sector and the image of the company.

TYPICAL COMMISSION RULES

1. Commission will be payable on all sales between 1 January and 31 December.
2. A 'sale' is defined as a signed contract from a client.
3. New client sales are defined as:
   - new sales from new clients;
   - new sales from new divisions or subsidiaries of existing clients;
   - new product sales to existing clients.

   A rate of X per cent will be paid for new sales.
4. Existing client sales are defined as repeat orders from existing clients. A rate of Y per cent will be paid for existing client repeat orders.
5. To claim commission the seller needs to attach supporting documentation (telesales report, letters sent, letters received, etc) to establish that, without the seller's intervention, the sale would not have happened.
6. The amount of the claim should be based on invoiced items, less purchase tax and any discounts granted.
7. Resignation will result in loss of commission for items invoiced after the letter of resignation is accepted.
8. Commission will be capped at £50,000 (or other relevant upper threshold) for any individual client.
9. Claims will be subject to quality audit and may be denied if minimum operating standards are not met.

With growing consumerism and a reduction in the cost-effectiveness of 'selling direct', excessive commission as a viable way to promote higher performance will become less defensible. Consumers will demand more service-orientated marketing.

PERFORMANCE-RELATED PAY (PRP)

Linking pay to performance is not the prerogative of sales or customer-facing staff. Many governments support the idea that there should be a regular and direct link between remuneration and standards of service. The argument goes that people will be more motivated if their remuneration is linked in some way to their performance (just like traditional sales people).

A proliferation of ways to achieve this sprang up: profit share; team pay; share ownership/options; gainsharing; profit-related pay; skill and competence pay; merit pay, and so on. Some schemes offer tax-free income for compliance with specific tax authority regulations. Others are devised by the sponsoring company to kick in when a certain level of company profit before tax is achieved or a predetermined operating standard is attained. Some companies have used the concept as a means to break the annual cycle of expectation, where employees receive an annual increment with an extra bit for merit, if the company can afford it. It can mean no annual increments. Increases are determined by company performance against budget or market share.

Provided the parameters are clearly set out and participating individuals understand how they can influence the result, PRP can be an effective way to communicate and emphasize the message that everyone can contribute to the greater good.

Disadvantages of PRP

However, this is rarely the case. Schemes triggered by residual profit often fall flat because the means to effect the profit equation (fewer overheads/more revenue) are not easy to calculate and communicate except at the year end. Within large corporations, profit levels may depend more on inter-group charges or local subsidies than any cost-cutting or efficiencies the employees may undertake. If you cannot as an individual see how your personal performance can make a difference, you are unlikely to change your behaviour. You are certainly not going to change the way you work for less than a 5 per cent take-home bonus.

In addition such schemes tend to attract arcane methods of calculation known only to the finance department, and the amount of profit share available is as much a surprise to the company directors as it is to the mail room. The extra money is duly pocketed some months after the end of the year (official audits need to be carried out to verify the final, year-end figures), by which time no one can remember what behaviour they are being rewarded for. The profit-related bonus becomes a post-dated reward rather than a dynamic incentive to promote performance improvement.

By their very nature such schemes tend to produce a relatively low reward as a percentage of salary (less than 5 per cent), which is not enough to promote a change in behaviour for the following year from most individuals. Various studies suggest that at least 10 per cent of take-home pay is necessary to activate a fundamental change of behaviour, particularly among middle-management salaried staff who have already reached their 'comfort level'.

MONEY – THE WORST MOTIVATOR

So why do we use 'more money' so often as an incentive only to be disappointed by its lacklustre effect? When you ask individuals in organizations the basic question which type of reward would motivate them to work harder, the top answer is always more money. (See Table 5.2.)

Cash is regularly surveyed, and is perceived to be the most effective incentive to encourage improved performance. Travel comes next, followed by various types of merchandise. However, as a means to encourage performance improvement,

Table 5.2 Reward media – percentage of companies using them

Reward medium	Percentage
Cash	43
Overseas travel	35
Vouchers	23
Merchandise	20
UK breaks	16
Sports events	14

Source: P&MM Group.

cash does have severe limitations. One of the most telling research findings about PRP comes from a study by Jenson and Murphy, University of Rochester, cited by US *Business Week*, in which the researchers compared the relationship between pay and overall corporate performance. After analysing the performance of 2,000 executives across 1,200 different companies in the United States they concluded there was no real correlation between PRP and company performance, and what's more, 'executives tend to be overpaid for bad performance and underpaid for good performance'.

A follow-up study by Berlet and Cravens covering 163 US companies also concluded that the link between executive PRP and a company's performance was virtually random. An Institute of Manpower study in the United Kingdom found that PRP by itself not only failed to improve staff performance but actually led to a 'downward spiral of demotivation', if customer demand was poor. A general view was held that whatever effort you put in could not change a flat market into a buoyant market. Unless you are operating in a continuous boom economic cycle, share options tend to disappoint as values go up and down with the market. Such rewards are not reliable and therefore not very useful as performance improvement incentives.

There comes a point when all managements ask the same questions about money. Why doesn't throwing more money at performance problems work, especially when even the staff say that more money is what they want? Beyond the employees' comfort zone, how can a manager motivate staff to make that extra effort? Why does cash seem to exhibit ever-diminishing returns?

Victor Vroom: work and motivation, 1964

One of the seminal experts on the effect of cash was Victor Vroom. He discovered that once a specific comfort level had been reached, offering more money in return for improved performance actually impaired performance as it created unproductive stress. It reinforced the view of the workforce that management can only think of staff as economic units, to be manipulated like plant and machinery to create higher profits.

Management teams that were perceived to motivate purely with money formulae were regarded as cynical and uncaring. By setting ever-increasing performance criteria linked solely to ever-higher cash amounts, employers created high levels of stress and anxiety, to the point that some individuals refused to participate any further and withdrew their (until that point) willing cooperation.

A self-fulfilling prophecy

The preponderance of cash as a motivator is so widespread in Western industrialized society that it begs the deeper question why it is used so often if it actually creates diminishing returns. As already suggested in Chapter 2, those who rise to positions of power tend to value money as the most important measure of worth and efficiency, particularly in entrepreneurial companies – a theory developed through several studies about the motivational effect of money. This leads to a propensity to use cash as a means to reward higher performance rather than other managerial techniques or non-cash rewards. Research carried out by Professor E R White shows that the psychological profile of successful entrepreneurs tends to perpetuate the idea that money or its accumulation is everyone's major driving force. More money becomes a self-fulfilling prophecy as a means to motivating people. If it works for me, the boss, it should work for everyone else, shouldn't it?

In other words, people have been subjected to extra cash for so long and so often as an incentive that participants feel it must be what they want, otherwise why would it be offered so relentlessly in their working lives, whatever their job?

Mazda Motor Of America, Inc

When Mazda Motor of America was planning an incentive to motivate Mazda dealers to sell B-Series trucks, Mazda's 900 dealerships were sharply divided on what kind of incentive would work best to improve sales from its 2,000 sales managers and 6,000 sales people. Some were adamant that only cash would shift the 'metal' from the forecourt. Others favoured non-cash awards such as merchandise or travel. A trip to Aspen, Colorado was offered to the top 15 sales managers, but the decision whether to offer sales people cash or something tangible such as merchandise or retail vouchers was still not resolved.

Upper management at Mazda were leaning towards offering more money, but decided to test the theory that non-cash works better than cash by initiating a straight split. Half the dealers were enrolled into a scheme in which they could earn cash, in this case around $75 per sale. The other half were offered a multi-level merchandise/travel product called AwardperQs whereby winners could choose their own reward items, depending on their performance. To add to the excitement participants were invited to call a toll-free number after each sale to claim a randomly distributed reward, either in cash or in AwardperQs. The rewards ranged anywhere from US~$10 to US~$250. This 'spin and win' format was quite common at the time within the automotive industry, as even one unit sale could end up with the participant 'hitting it big'.

The results were astonishing. The non-cash group consistently achieved higher sales levels throughout the campaign period, and this was true regardless of the size of the dealership. At the end of the campaign the cash group had only managed a 2.13 per cent increase over their sales objective, whereas the non-cash group had achieved a 15.65 per cent increase.

Post-campaign research revealed that the low-volume dealers were not enthused by just $75 for every additional truck sold, as they calculated that they would not be able to sell enough extra volume to make it worthwhile after deductions. However, those in the non-cash group could clearly identify in personal and family terms what the rewards would be, and worked towards that goal, almost regardless of its monetary value. Mazda's own post-campaign research concluded, 'A reasonable assumption is that the emotional impact of an offer of tangible rewards i.e. merchandise and travel, is more powerful from a behavioural-change point of view, than is an offer of an equivalent sum of money.'

Trophy value

An aspect of money as a poor motivator is its inherent lack of image. It has no 'trophy' value. People do not like to talk about how much extra money they have earned in a given period to friends and relatives, although they will talk about being given a letter of commendation or being taken out to dinner by the boss or receiving an invitation to a prestigious overseas travel event, or some other non-cash privilege. It is simply not socially acceptable to boast openly about how much you earned last month. Also, money tends to be absorbed into everyday expenses, and once paid electronically into the bank merges with the rest of the monthly income. Its use as a reminder of a job well done is soon forgotten, both for employee and employer.

As society in general becomes more affluent, most people in employment are not living on or below the poverty line. Most people are able to generate slightly more income over their regular expenditure beyond pure subsistence, so additional cash income is a less powerful motivator to change behaviour. People have achieved a comfort zone to the extent that the extra effort to accumulate more money is not worth the incremental pain of achieving it.

Table 5.3   What cash costs the company

Cost differential on £100	Cash	Non-cash
Original award	£100	£100
Employer's National Insurance contribution at 12.8%	£16	£15
Tax at 22%, if employer grosses up	£28	£27
Market discount (5%)	Nil	(Less £5)
Total cost to employer	£144	£137

Example based on basic rate taxpayer.

Cash is expensive

Cash is usually more expensive for corporations to provide as a reward or incentive medium than non-cash. Under the United Kingdom's fiscal regime, cash is 5 per cent more expensive. A combination of slightly lower tax rates and the discount normally available for non-cash items has resulted in some employer savings by avoiding cash altogether. (See table 5.3.)

As for the participant, if the employee opted for a cash payment on which tax would be due rather than a non-cash payment on which the tax would already have been paid, the difference in 'income' could be substantial.

So not only does the company pay more if it opts to reward with cash, but also the individual receives less if he or she is rewarded with cash. It all adds up to a bad deal for both the giver and the receiver. (See table 5.4.)

Table 5.4   What the participant takes home

Income differential on £100	Cash (taxed)	Non-cash (tax pre-paid)
Original award	£100	£100
Less employee's National Insurance contribution at 11%	£11	£11
Less tax at 22%	£22	N/A
Amount received by participant	£67	£89

In summary, these are the disadvantages of cash:

- It is more expensive than non-cash.
- It has little trophy value or memorability for recipients.
- It suggests the company is cynical and manipulative (and devoid of imagination).
- It is an easy, but ineffective option, especially for employees in the comfort zone.

But if you are stuck with a cash incentive scheme for whatever reason, you can still make more of it if you have to use cash as a motivational lever despite the inherent disadvantages. A national parcels and documents delivery company had been running a monthly cash bonus scheme for its workforce for many years. Each month on their pay slip, employees would receive an amount of extra money for 'performance'. Unfortunately no one, except the financial director, knew what the performance criteria were. So the original objective to improve performance quickly became a retrospective reward for historical achievements which remained largely mysterious. This was a classic case of an innovative idea strangled by the payment process.

What this company needed to do was communicate with the workforce how the monthly sum was calculated and explain what the performance measures were, so that participants could at least try to match last month's performance, if not better it. It transpired during the research phase that the formula for payment was based on divisional profitability factored by current salary. As a system it certainly ensured that rewards were linked directly to profits, but there was no link to the everyday working practices of the employees.

A long hard look was taken at what people actually did and what constituted 'good performance'. Delivery drivers, for example, were asked how they thought their performance might be best measured. They suggested such elements as timekeeping, getting legible acceptance signatures from clients, delivering jobs on time, planning the call cycle, and asking for additional orders. This process continued with the clerical staff and the sales force. At the end of the investigation period it proved relatively simple to devise regular communication for each individual showing his or her personal performance against key tasks and hence the cash bonus level. Once participants could link their behaviour to the reward, performance of even basic tasks improved dramatically.

Money or a massage?

Here is an example of not always believing what people say when it comes to money, but acting on what they actually do. Scott Jeffrey, assistant professor of management sciences based at the University of Waterloo, Ontario published in the magazine *Salesforcexp*, October 2004 the results of an experiment undertaken at the University of Chicago. Participants were invited to take part in a word game on campus in pursuit of an incentive. One group was rewarded with cash. The other group qualified for a therapeutic massage of varying length, depending on their performance. The market values of the rewards were equal. The massage group, after the experiment, was then asked whether they would have preferred the cash to the massage, and 78 per cent said they would. However, the analysis of relative performances revealed that although the cash group performed 14.6 per cent better than the no-incentive control group, the massage group performed 38.6 per cent better than the cash group, over twice as big an improvement.

Further follow-up questions showed that the participants found it difficult to justify spending the cash on a massage but would be perfectly happy to receive a massage as a reward alternative. The study suggests overall that tangible incentives for employees should be aspirational items, in other words things they would not normally purchase for themselves. Participants will often say they would work hardest for money, but studies show they actually perform better when offered tangibles, all other factors being equal.

Money is not the only answer

The advice is clearly not to outlaw money completely as a motivator. That would be nonsense. But it has to be put in its rightful place if the discussion is about effective incentives. Money will certainly reward people for as historic job done well (or even adequately) and provide basic security, but it rarely works as well as non-cash rewards if you are looking for improved or incremental performance.

SUMMARY

- Salary, commission and PRP have their place in rewarding historic performance.
- But cash costs more to provide than non-cash.
- Beyond an employee's comfort zone, cash exhibits diminishing returns.
- More money is the least efficient and effective motivator.

---

6 | Flexible benefits

The chief value of money is that one lives in a world in which it is over estimated.

H L Mencken

You are now armed with an understanding of motivation techniques and have considered the merits or otherwise of cash versus non-cash, but you still have one corporate financial hurdle to clear before you can start to use tangibles or non-cash rewards. What about the 30 per cent or more of the annual salary bill paid out in benefits of various kinds, from life assurance to childcare vouchers? Surely this represents a major opportunity to promote performance improvement using a financial commitment which already exists? But the problem is that few employers know exactly who is getting what at any moment in time, especially in larger companies where details of individual benefits may be held by different departments in a variety of formats. For benefits to be used as a performance incentive or loyalty reward, the employer needs to get a clear view of who is receiving what amount of benefit on an individual basis, otherwise how can you set any form of individual benchmark? But how effective is this spend, and does it actually motivate people to work harder or stay in a job for longer than they otherwise would?

Benefits do not fall neatly into Herzberg's two-factor theory of motivation. Benefits can be both satisfiers or dissatisfiers. Depending on how the benefits are communicated, the employer could be either wasting the investment or reaping a huge improvement bonus. The key factor is whether employees perceive their benefits or perks as valuable or simply part of their rightful remuneration. Are benefits as elusive as cash when it comes to their motivational effectiveness or potential?

The first questions to ask are, what are employment benefits and why is there a mood of change sweeping through the advanced industrialized nations to reappraise the value and proportion of benefits as part of an employee's total remuneration package?

BENEFITS AS SECURITY

In the last three generations, the world has experienced two global wars, nuclear physics, the establishment and collapse of Soviet communism, and varying degrees of individual freedom within an increasingly industrialized society. These factors have conspired to produce a general acceptance that the employer as well as the state has a duty to provide a certain degree of financial security and stability. In some companies in the late 19th century this manifested itself in worker communities set up and regulated by the company to ensure loyalty and a reliable source of labour. Because they cocooned employees in subsidized housing, offered social facilities and provided other supportive systems, employees began to expect that the employer should take on a paternal as well as an economic role. Victorian patriarchs were known for being strict but fair. Those employers who did not provide non-cash support were perceived as old-fashioned and exploitative. So strong was the pressure that eventually legislation ensured that some employment benefits became statutory rather than optional. The concept of the 'nanny state' was born.

Clearly, within the context of social history this was a good idea: less worker exploitation, higher living standards, more job stability, and competition between employers to deliver a bigger and better remuneration package to attract skilled and semi-skilled employees alike. But times change. Although many employees now enjoy a range of benefits never dreamt of by their grandparents, questions are being asked about whether today's employees really appreciate their value. Western employers are asking whether such benefits can be justified in a global market where many Third World suppliers do not, as yet, carry the heavy burden of all this accumulated expectation of employee benefits. Younger employees are also questioning the relevance of such mandatory benefits as pension contributions and life assurance when they have only a vague appreciation of their ultimate value.

BENEFITS AS LOYALTY INCENTIVES

A solution seems to be presenting itself. Why not give people benefits which match their individual situation? Let them choose what they want. An answer was developed to meet this need, in the form of core benefits, voluntary additional benefits and eventually flexible benefits or 'flex plans'. Initially such flexibility of benefits options was only granted to senior executives, but the demand from lower down the hierarchy has been so great that now many junior employees take advantage of benefits choice.

Born in the United States from the need to control the spiralling cost of health care, US employers began to offer 'flex' as a means of reducing overall cost exposure and recognizing employee diversity. In the late 1980s Chrysler calculated that up to US$800 per car went on employee benefits. Something had to be done to reduce this increasing cost problem. In Western Europe, most companies offer a limited range of financial products designed to cater for major life events: life assurance; pensions; sickness or disability benefit. In the United States, Canada, South Africa and more recently Australia, the concept has been expanded to include a whole range of benefits in the drive to give employers more control of company expenditure, and the employee more choice and value for money, with a possible spin-off, in terms of recruitment and improved loyalty.

Europe is not far behind. The United Kingdom leads the market but Ireland and Spain are developing fast. Countries with strong unions and less flexible legislation when it comes to employee benefits, such as France, Italy and Germany, are less enthusiastic. But if and when the European Union is ever able to agree on a common employee benefits policy, in the effort to promote flexibility in the EU labour market, it is likely that flex plans will play a key role in allowing nationals to work anywhere in the EU with the minimum of financial disruption.

In the United Kingdom, according to a survey conducted jointly by the magazine *Employee Benefits* and financial specialist Chase de Vere in 2004, 15 per cent of UK employers with more than 100 staff offered employees some form of flexible benefits scheme, and almost half stated that in the future most employers will have to be able to offer the facility if they want to compete for the best skills in the marketplace.

Types of benefit plan

Before flex plans came along many large organizations provided relatively simple benefits packages according to status or length of service. Following the Victorian model, everyone typically received some kind of life assurance, with the option to contribute towards a pension plan. As 'core' benefits these non-cash elements were not negotiable but simply offered as part of the remuneration package. As organizations grew the administration of these arrangements became increasingly complex, especially if employees were transferred to other branches or even overseas. In addition, it became clear to employers that by buying financial products in bulk, there were substantial savings to be made which could be passed on to staff and used as a loyalty incentive when it came to improving retention in a competitive job market. Administration was outsourced to actuarially based consultants who took over the reporting and communication of benefits in return for a fee. 'Total reward statements' were produced for employees so they could see what benefits they were entitled to.

It did not take long for employers to realize that they could offer other financial advantages to staff by buying items and services in bulk. Alternatively they could allow staff to upgrade their core benefits beyond the initial package at their own expense. The concept of voluntary benefits was born. As an employee, you could get significant discounts on everyday items, if the organization did a deal with the relevant suppliers. 'Employee savings' schemes were then developed with often hundreds of suppliers. Staff could choose to simply take advantage of the discounts or use some of their salary to make discounted purchases.

ITV Deals: an employee voluntary discount scheme

ITV, the television company, wanted to enhance the range of discounted voluntary benefits available to its 17,000 employees and pensioners, and to communicate them through accessible and low-maintenance means. Part of the thinking was to offer a range of discounts on products and services that fitted with the lifestyles and interests of its relatively young workforce, and to communicate the ITV branded scheme online, as well as on paper, making the benefits accessible from both work and home.

It commissioned an external supplier, Motivano, to procure the discounted products and provide the communication material, including an ITV Deals website which employees can access via the ITV intranet or at home via the internet. (See Figure 6.1.) All the communication materials were designed in conjunction with ITV's brand designers to ensure that the products sourced by Motivano were clearly communicated as an ITV employee benefit in a way that fitted with the corporate brand. Access to the website was direct via a password, and all new joiners would receive the *ITV Deals* magazine and membership card as and when they were recruited during the year. There were regular printed newsletters, e-mail messages and special deals announced throughout the year.

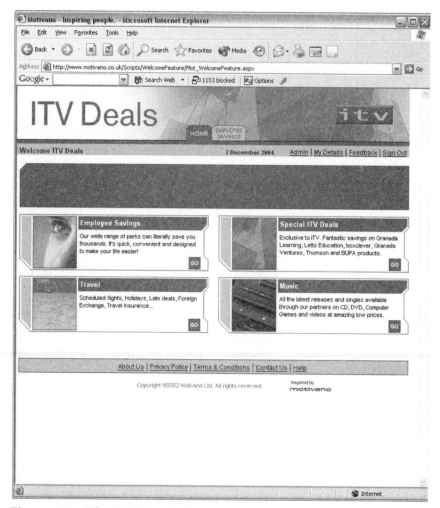

Figure 6.1 The ITV Deals home screen

The key element of the scheme was the administration of discounts across a wide range of suppliers. They included insurance and finance, travel and holidays, hotels, car hire, books and magazines, health clubs, leisure options, music, food and drink, home furnishings and gardens, toys, fashion and beauty among many others. Discounts ranged from 10 per cent to 40 per cent for some products in the range. (See Figure 6.2.)

An important element was the ability to access the site from home, thereby involving the whole family in the choice of savings

Figure 6.2   ITV Deals typical offers

to be made. There is no doubt that the promotional possibilities provided by offering a selection of employee savings in addition to core benefits helps to keep the issue of benefits for employees high on the agenda. ITV Deals enables all employees to take advantage of some very good deals as a result of working for ITV. And as a result, this scheme reinforces to employees the benefits they get from working at ITV, which helps to retain staff and keep them loyal.

With the advent of flexible benefits, the wheel came full circle. Now staff could adjust the proportion of cash to benefits they received in a variety of ways to suit their own lifestyle. New employees could be offered a remuneration package expressed in cash or credits and then opt how they wanted to be paid. The key change was the emergence of the software to do the job inexpensively and efficiently. In addition, using the software would require the client to have a robust intranet, and be used to communicating online as part of their everyday business dealings.

Not all schemes fit this development model. Some large organizations still use paper-based reporting, rather than their intranet, for various security reasons. Others only allow certain levels of staff to 'flex fully' as a device to encourage retention. Others still simply offer discount cards as their response to staff diversity. However, there is no doubt that flexible benefits are here to stay and likely to become the standard way to remunerate employees in the future.

What are the choices of benefit?

It is clear from the list in Table 6.1 that individuals want different types of benefit at varying levels. The tax regime in each country may also determine which benefits represent good value in that particular economic and legislative environment.

You can imagine what benefits individuals might prefer, depending on their personal circumstances. But it is difficult and dangerous to predict what employees want without full consultation. Every workforce is different.

However, there are some common main drivers for employees when it comes to benefit choice, although most choices reflect what is uppermost in the minds of employees when the choice is

Table 6.1 What is meant by benefits?

Money	Health/family	Insurance	Other
Salary	Health	Life	Mobile phone
Share/stock	screening	assurance	Home
options	Dental care	Pension	computer
Credit card	Eye care	Disability	Car
subscriptions	Counselling	insurance	Car parking
Interest on loans	(legal/personal)	Critical	Private fuel
Short-term	Creche	illness cover	Non-
savings plan	School fees	Accident	vocational
Housing subsidy	Childcare	cover	training
Financial	vouchers	Short-term	Luncheon
planning	Elderly parent	sick pay	vouchers
	support	Household	Subsidized
	Sports and	insurance	restaurant
	social facilities	Motor	Relocation
		insurance	Holidays

offered. The survey mentioned above identified buying/selling leave days as the most popular traded benefit, followed by childcare vouchers, critical illness insurance, dental insurance and a private health care plan, in that order of preference. This clearly reflects the stated drivers of benefit choice.

DRIVERS OF BENEFIT CHOICE

- More time off.
- Loss of health.
- Making ends meet (more cash).
- Flexibility if circumstances change.
- Value for money.
- Security.
- Prospects of advancement.
- Status (both perceived and actual).

The important thing is to ask employees what they would prefer, given the choice, although some care should be taken in the research process not to set up expectations that cannot be delivered when the new scheme is launched. However it is always useful to know what other people in other schemes have chosen. A survey of the market by IDS (Incomes Data Services) in 2003 revealed the following popularity of benefits choices in the United Kingdom:

Most common flexible benefits

- childcare vouchers;
- critical illness insurance;
- dental insurance;
- holidays;
- life assurance;
- permanent health insurance;
- personal accident insurance;
- private medical insurance;
- travel insurance.

Fairly common flexible benefits

- car;
- health cash plan;
- health screening;
- pensions;
- retail vouchers.

Less common flexible benefits

- car breakdown cover;
- financial planning;
- health club membership;
- legal protection insurance;
- lifestyle management services;
- personal computer leasing;
- pet insurance;
- will writing.

Employee types

All employees are not the same, as the following examples show. But even those listed below are stereotypes and may not match your own workforce profile. Indeed, one employee's ideal benefits package may not meet the needs of another employee, who may be at the same grade, doing the same job.

---

1. SINGLE, UNDER 30 YEARS OLD

- Disposable income.
- Disability insurance.
- Extra-curricular training.
- Meal subsidies.
- Sports facilities.
- Mobile phone.
- Car.

---

2. MARRIED WOMAN WITH YOUNG CHILDREN, WORKING PART-TIME

- Sick pay.
- Life assurance.
- Childcare vouchers.
- Holidays.
- Health screening.
- Housing subsidy.
- Medical insurance.
- Creche.

---

3. MARRIED MAN, 45 YEARS OLD, MAIN FAMILY BREADWINNER

- Life assurance.
- Pension.
- Disability insurance.

- Eye care.
- Dental care.
- Housing subsidy.
- Credit card subscriptions.
- Car.

These deliberate caricatures illustrate the advantage of flexible benefits. Each individual is given, as part of his or her remuneration package, a specific number of 'credits' which can be spent, to varying degrees, on any or all the benefits on offer, or indeed be converted into cash. For many benefits it will depend on the value of money as perceived by the employee whether they will be more or less prized as part of remuneration. But the principle is sound: free choice, according to your personal circumstances. Because there can be significant cost savings in buying some benefits in bulk, or because the employer feels a moral obligation to protect employees in cases of hardship (life assurance, health care), many schemes include a number of 'core' benefits which everyone receives up to a minimum level.

Defined costs

There is a significant advantage to the employer here, and that is cost control. In other words, employers can move to a 'defined cost' for benefits rather than the open-ended cost so characteristic of many current non-flex benefit schemes. For the employee it is value for money. Perhaps for the first time, by going through the process of creating a flex plan, the employer will have identified what benefits are valued by each individual employee. It can represent a finite cost within the company budget, but as most benefits are individually costed, there will be different benchmark figures for each age group or business unit. When new recruits are taken on, or package negotiations are taking place with more senior-level appointments, there is no longer any need to horse-trade on various benefits. The package could include 30 per cent or more 'in benefits'. Negotiations can be about the percentage range, but there is no need to wonder whether offering a better car or a bigger pension allocation will do the trick or be in conflict with peer group employees. That decision is left to the employee. It removes all the status anomalies so prevalent when you compare senior management packages even within specific industries, and allows the human resources department to budget its spend more accurately. In the UK market, where benefits for senior appointments could be over 50 per cent of salary, more accuracy on expenditure is a welcome tool for sound management of overheads.

In the United Kingdom there has been much more openness about executive remuneration in recent years, leading to more and more transparency concerning benefits, and this will eventually feed into more communication when it comes to what more junior employees receive as remuneration. People want to know more about the actual cost of benefits, and demand is growing from the workforce to be able to choose the benefits that suit them and their lifestyle.

So much for theory, what about the practice?

Some very big companies have already gone the flexible benefits route, including PepsiCo Foods International, Colgate Palmolive, Prudential, Royal Mail, Cadbury Schweppes and Hitachi Europe. But not all of them have included every employee in their schemes. Each company had its own cultural problems to overcome. All realized that sound advice, good internal communication and administrative excellence are required to introduce the change successfully.

Key stages of 'flexing'

There are some key practical issues to bear in mind before becoming a born-again 'flexer'. There are many unforeseen variables which need careful consideration before overhauling such a high item of the overheads. Getting it wrong could mean the company risks raising expectations it cannot deliver, making it impossible to raise the flexible benefits issue in the future.

PRACTICAL POINTS

- Pinpoint the strategic reasons for switching to a flex plan.
- Study competitor activity.
- Get commitment from senior management and unions.
- Start the dialogue with providers.
- Consult with employees.
- Build and test a working model.
- Communicate with employees.
- Examine the tax and insurance issues carefully.
- Plan for additional administration.
- Amend in the light of experience.

There is a current trend towards using a significant part of salary to buy benefits and there is certainly less emphasis on limiting employees to a nominal flex fund. The design of your scheme should reflect this trend. In some countries there are substantial tax and National Insurance savings to be made when flexing is incorporated into a salary sacrifice scheme. Often these savings can fund the cost of administering the scheme. Flex plan models are now available for all staff, not just senior managers, so consider carefully how far down the organization you can go. Due to the developments in software which have taken place only in the last few years, flex plans can now be offered to small organizations too, so they are no longer the preserve of large multinationals.

Probably most important of all, get professional advice to guide you through these stages, even if you decide to do most of the internal research and development yourself. A useful guide to UK suppliers can be found in the Directory of Suppliers as part of the Incomes Data Services Ltd brochure number 762 entitled 'IDS studies plus – flexible benefits, 2003'.

Flexing for the right reasons

Many accountancy-based management consultancies will argue that flex plans can deliver increased staff retention and therefore lower recruitment costs in the future. This has never been proved, although the argument is a compelling one. Being more competitive when it comes to establishing remuneration benchmarks is certainly one of the bonuses of a flex plan, but there are more important things at stake. It is better to view things, at least initially, from a more strategic viewpoint.

A flex plan needs to be consistent with your company's strategic aims. If part of your strategy for personnel includes more empowerment, reducing layers of management, creating a flatter structure or simply responding to company cultural changes demanding more individual choice, then a flex plan could be part of the answer. If you have a diverse workforce which typically includes a number of 'time servers' as well as self-motivated high flyers, then a flex plan provides the opportunity to meet the needs of both groups in a single scheme.

For a modern, hi-tech employer which prides itself on creativity, innovation, team spirit and being seen to reward loyalty, a flex plan is one way to express this philosophy. If you genuinely feel that 30 per cent or more of your personnel overheads could be better utilized as a business investment by offering a personal choice of benefits rather than a standard package, then a flex plan provides distinct advantages.

But if your main aim is to reduce immediately the level of benefits you feel obliged to provide as a percentage of your overheads, because you want to raise profitability, then flex is not the answer. If you have an ageing workforce in a mature industry and want to avoid expensive final salary pension pay-offs, you would be better advised to talk to a pensions specialist, rather than expect a flex plan to deliver lower costs. If you think you already know what is best for your workforce in terms of benefits, a flex plan will offer you no advantages.

Flex plans are about corporate personnel strategy and assessing the motivational value of benefits rather than a quick fix to avoid future liabilities or reduce current costs. Once the board, with its advisers, has decided that a flex plan could deliver relevant advantages and is consistent with the company's personnel strategy, the next step is consultation with your employees.

Developing the plan

In an ideal world, agreement should be sought and the plan developed in consultation with those employees who will be affected. In the present state of development of flex plans this is likely initially to be senior employees with substantial packages. This echelon makes up the bulk of current flex plan participants. But there are more and more company-wide schemes being introduced, particularly within US subsidiaries. A recent survey revealed that 15 per cent of all UK companies operate some form of flexible benefits package, with a further 64 per cent expressing serious interest. Care is needed to explain to employees current benefits and the impact of the new benefits, both initially and in the longer term.

It is normal for a feasibility plan to be drawn up, which involves establishing a project team to look at the various issues. The team should include representatives of those employee groups likely to be affected, as well as representatives from the technical areas (information processing, administration, senior management). Allocate adequate time to the planning phase to get early views aired and misconceptions clarified. Most flex plans need at least 12 months' gestation.

With the consultation process under way, the project team can move forward to an outline design – what choices to offer, when to introduce the plan, how to communicate the scheme – with a view to implementation. At some stage unions will need to be involved, the earlier the better. Experience to date has shown that unions tend to view flex plans with suspicion until they can see it is in the employees' interest to have choice. Provided nothing is being taken away, flex plans represent in broad terms a neutral change, in terms of budget, and therefore should be welcomed by unions and workforce alike. You may decide, if the company is big enough, that a pilot test would be appropriate to see what can be learned from a limited implementation process. In the United Kingdom the initial step is often to flex existing benefits by reducing them to a cash sum which employees then use to 'buy back' their benefits in the same or different proportions. In effect a flex plan formalizes the initiative of offering choice of how much of each benefit to take, although in theory the actual overhead cost will be the same to the employer.

Check out assumptions

Assumptions about what people want or their understanding of the concept should be cross-checked, and senior management should always avoid the temptation to 'steamroller' an agreement through. The consultation process should not simply be an administrative rubber stamp. There may be sound reasons for changing the choice of benefits, changing the timetable for their introduction or delaying the introduction of flex indefinitely. What may seem right for the board may not be right for employees lower down, so automatic acceptance of the concept should not be assumed for all levels.

A genuine consultation process will improve the take-up of the scheme and create new ideas from potential participants to facilitate its operation. The more participant ownership there is, the more successful the scheme will be. But be prepared for a quiet and cautious start – most people have difficulty imagining how new concepts work in practice. If the intention is to provide new contracts for everybody, but with largely the same benefits as before, you might expect up to 80 per cent or more participation, with the balance joining in during year two. The experience of consultants in the flex plan area shows that if the scheme is professionally introduced, participants make dramatic inputs in years two and three, once they have experienced and understood the advantages. At this point, you need to take care that natural enthusiasm does not lead the company into expensive administration routines or agreeing to additional benefits it cannot deliver, or cannot pay for out of current or future profits. In particular, the option to save holiday days or buy more holiday days is difficult for people to plan over the long term. They may not want to commit to this concept six months out from when they plan to save or take the holiday.

Flex plan example

A major telecommunications company suggested that the communication strategy of implementing its flex plan was crucial in its successful introduction and in gathering intelligence about how it could improve the way it got the features of the plan across to future employees. The scheme involved over 10,000 employees.

The standard benefits package for all employees on permanent contracts includes 25 days' annual leave, free private medical insurance, an employee assistance programme (EAP), a save-as-you-earn scheme offering company shares, an employee bonus scheme, discounted telephone and personal insurance products, and a competitive final salary pension scheme. The company spends over £50 million per annum on employment benefits in order to attract and retain the calibre of employee necessary to support the strategic goals of the business. It was felt that further improvements could be made to this benefits programme: first by making employees aware of how much the company was spending on their behalf (a fact which is often not brought to employees' attention); and secondly by introducing an element of choice to the benefits programme.

The workforce, like many, reflects a considerable social range, and it was felt that the benefits programme was the one key feature of the employment process that did not include provision for the individual. For example, the appraisal, career development, training and remuneration policies all include the individual as a key factor, but the benefits programme tends to assume that everyone is the same. Flexible benefits were therefore developed to address these issues.

An internal feasibility study investigated the actual cost of benefits provision take-up, opportunities for flexing, which employees should be covered, tax, systems and pricing issues. A desk study of newly introduced UK flex schemes was carried out, and four companies agreed to participate in the research and provide information during interviews. A number of senior managers were interviewed about flex and the results were very positive.

Because the flex programme is on a comparatively large scale it was decided to introduce the idea to a pilot group of employees in advance of the main launch. This was done not only to test out the administration, systems and communications aspects, but also because the employees had not been consulted and this would enable feedback before the main launch. Flex was introduced to a pilot group of 400 employees principally in the research and development area. The programme was positioned as additional to the existing benefit entitlements, and employees were able to choose whether or not they wished to take part. The response was very positive: 34 per cent of employees chose to vary their benefit provision and the general reaction was encouraging.

The benefits positioned within the flex programme are pension, life cover, health care, dental insurance, annual leave, car and childcare. Not all of these were available for the pilot group but some have been introduced since. All flex options are designed to be cost-neutral. Employees decide if they want to have the options and must commit to receiving their choice for a 12-month period.

Pension

Employees in the pension scheme accrue retirement pension at the rate of 60ths for each year of service. This costs the employee 5 per cent of pensionable salary. Flex offers four new options, where employees are able to trade up in order to accrue pension at a faster rate, and either plan for early retirement or improve their existing pension potential. These are 55ths, 50ths, 45ths and 40ths. Employees can contribute up to a total of 15 per cent of salary, depending on factors such as how much they can afford, their age and past pension provision. The pension choices proved popular for the employees in the pilot group; 10 per cent of employees bought better pension cover.

Life cover

Employees in the pension scheme receive life cover of four times their pensionable salary. Employees outside the scheme receive no life cover. Flex recognizes that all employees may not want four times cover, and allows those in the pension scheme to trade down to three or two times cover and receive a cash credit instead. Employees not in the pension scheme can buy up to two, three or four times cover at the same rates.

Health care

Health care is provided free to employees on the basis of their family status: single employees receive single cover, married employees receive married cover and so on. These employees are now able to trade down on the cover for their partner and dependants, and receive a cash credit instead. This may be of particular benefit to an employee whose partner already receives private medical insurance at his or her place of work. Flex also includes an opportunity for employees to trade up to a higher-level health care scheme with a higher financial limit for outpatient care. In addition, the company arranged for employees to have a private medical health screen at a discounted rate. This cost is met by the employee.

Dental insurance

The company currently offers a single-level dental scheme which provides reimbursement at NHS levels. Flex introduces an alternative plan providing reimbursement at private treatment cost levels. These costs are met by the employee, but are available at rates below those of external plans.

Annual leave

The company offers 25 working days' leave to permanent full-time employees, but the flex programme will enable employees to vary their leave by up to 5 working days each year. Employees can therefore trade down to 20 days or up to 30. This choice requires the approval of the employee's line manager.

Employee cars

In addition to the existing company car scheme, which enables management employees to have a car of their choice, or a cash option, or a combination of the two, the company has introduced a lease-purchase car scheme which offers all employees a choice of virtually any new car at their own cost. This is operated by the companies that supply the business fleet, and offers an alternative to the high-street lease-purchase schemes.

Childcare vouchers

Vouchers are being launched with flex. They can be used to pay a nursery, childminder, nanny or similar, and are free of National Insurance. The employee must agree to relinquish a chosen portion of salary and will receive the vouchers instead. This will give most employees about a 6 per cent saving on childcare costs.

Flex packs

The flexible benefits programme is being communicated through presentations, posters, the company newspaper and 'flex packs' which contain each employee's personalized choices. These are sent to home addresses, because so many of the flex choices are family decisions. The enrolment process ran for 10 weeks. Flex then went live for all employees to receive independent external financial counselling to help them with their pension choices. This is available on a helpline and through 'surgeries' at various company locations.

Communication

Communicating about issues within companies rather than from business to business or from company to consumer is a growing discipline, but it is not growing fast enough. The normal rules of thumb for consumer marketing tend not to be translated across to internal staff even with consumer-driven companies, and consequently many worthy initiatives die on the vine because of a lack of serious internal communication. The investment in time and materials is rarely made, resulting in poorly perceived communication. You need to be clear what messages you wish to give and what response you are hoping for.

Ajilon: a communications case study

Formed in 2002, the Ajilon Group brings all of Adecco's niche recruitment brands in the UK together, providing permanent and temporary recruitment services via a number of organizations including Office Angels (administration and secretarial), Computer People (IT) and Jonathan Wren (banking and finance). Each company has its own identity and brand within its market niche, and naturally each one had a different benefits scheme. In bringing together the organizations Ajilon inherited different cultures, workforce compositions, structures, philosophies, terms and conditions, benefit offerings and providers. There was a strong need to harmonize the benefits and suppliers into one scheme so that all 1,300 employees could take advantage of the same range of benefits. In addition the company wanted to ensure that the benefits on offer were fully understood and appreciated across the group. The idea of a flex plan was also in keeping with Ajilon's positioning as a market leader and an innovator.

In terms of scheme design it decided that the programme should offer employee savings and discounts, voluntary benefits and the option, eventually, for employees to fully flex all the benefits within their individual packages. It invented a brand for the scheme called 'enjoy!' so that anyone within the group would recognize it as the umbrella term for the new benefits scheme. (See Figure 6.3.)

The programme was rolled out in phases so as not to overload staff with too much information all at once. (See Figure 6.4.) There were online teasers that gave an outline of the scheme being planned. The employee savings element, rebranded as Lifestyle, was announced first, and included a wide range of discounts from travel and holidays through to cinema tickets and clothes.

coming soon!
flexible benefits

We'll soon be launching Flexible Benefits, the third part of the Ajilon enjoy! programme. Under the new scheme, you'll be able to tailor your benefits package, exchanging the benefits that don't suit you, for the ones that do.

Building on core basics like life assurance, pension and BUPA, you can create your benefits around what's important to you - more holiday, a better pension, whatever. You'll also have access to benefits that haven't been available to you and your family before.

You can design a new package once a year and it's all done online so it's nice and simple. You can even do it on your home PC.

how will you use your flexible benefits?

- When you're young and single, your pension can seem like a lifetime away. You might want to cash in a portion of that benefit to take care of more immediate matters, like dental benefits to keep your smile healthy or insurance to cover sports-related injuries.
- If you've got loved ones depending on you, you might need to think about the bigger benefits picture. Exchanging a couple of holiday days could buy extra life assurance, pension or family health insurance... and extra peace of mind.

there's more to enjoy...

Don't forget, there are two other parts of the scheme to enjoy throughout the year -

Lifestyle benefits @ www.ajilonenjoy.co.uk - our very own benefits website offers deals on a host of products and services - from CD players to seaside holidays.

Voluntary benefits - using the buying power of Ajilon and Motivano (the company helping us put the enjoy! scheme together), we've arranged discounts on essentials like health screenings, dental and optical cover.

You'll receive more information through April and May.

AJILON GROUP BENEFITS

www.ajilonenjoy.co.uk

Figure 6.3 An introduction for employees to Ajilon's flex benefits scheme

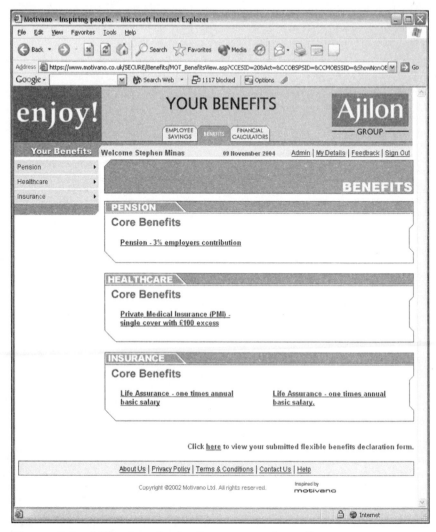

Figure 6.4 Ajilon's enjoy! scheme: core benefits

Following a survey of opinions, the second phase introduced a range of voluntary benefits at corporate rates to include medical and dental services, fitness and childcare vouchers and accident and illness insurance. (See Figure 6.5.)

Finally, the flexing facility was communicated through road-shows, deskdrops, letters to home addresses, brochures (see Figure 6.6), online communications and the establishment of

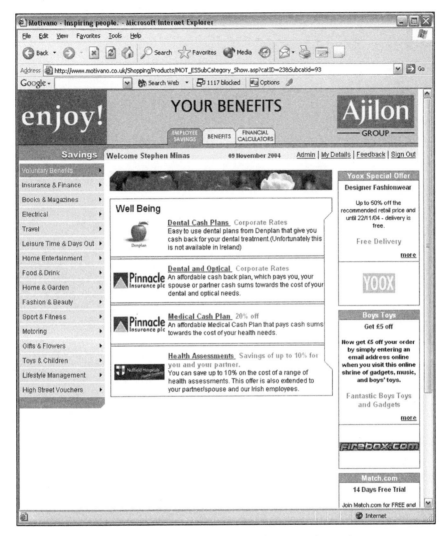

Figure 6.5   Ajilon's enjoy! scheme: voluntary benefits

'flex champions' throughout the organization to act as coordinators for any new initiatives and points of human contact for employees. A member of the marketing team joined the implementation project team to help overcome the problem of e-mail overload and was instrumental in thinking up new ways to communicate, such as putting posters on the back of toilet doors, for example.

Figure 6.6 The Ajilon enjoy! scheme brochure

Each member of staff had their total remuneration reconfigured to create core benefits, in this case life assurance, pensions and health care. The difference in value between the original value of their package became the flex allowance that they could now spend on a wide range of other benefits. Choice was the driving force behind reconfiguring the presentation of the revised benefits.

The post launch survey was very encouraging, with 80 per cent participation and an endorsement by 71 per cent of the participants that the new scheme was perceived to be better than the old scheme. In addition Ajilon was able to rationalize its purchase of benefits by using a central broker, already active in the marketplace, to further reduce costs and improve the discounts being made available to employees in the scheme.

THE STAGES OF EFFECTIVE COMMUNICATION

With all communication issues you need to consider the level of understanding of the audience (without being patronizing), the content of the message, the medium through which the message is communicated and the timing. Each audience may require a slightly different message on presentation. Each stage of the process may require a different approach. There will be a great deal to communicate at the beginning of the programme, but take care not to congratulate yourself on the amount of material you have produced. People may never get round to reading it, particularly younger, more mobile employees. The main points need to be emphasized verbally, with back-up literature for those who like to take in the information in their own time at their own pace. During the first year, a regular feature in the company newsletter or even an audio CD (radio programme style) on a regular basis can be used to feed back information to respond to some of the main misunderstandings or common queries. It can also be useful to feature testimonials from various types of employee so people can compare choices and discuss their relative merits. At the first and subsequent anniversaries, employees will be preparing to review their options. Face-to-face discussion should be encouraged to reassure those thinking about making some changes. Many companies find a 'clinic' approach helps people make better decisions.

The relative merits can be aired, either individually or in a group, with the help of a facilitator, from within the company or from a consultancy.

In this way employees will be happier with their eventual choices and take a real interest in the value of each benefit to their particular current situation. The theory of cognitive dissonance – buyers needing reassurance that they have made the right choice – applies with flex plan choices. Remember to reassure choosers.

SOME COMMON COMMUNICATION ERRORS

- Failure to do enough research.
- Raising expectations in the research phase which cannot be delivered.
- Too much information too quickly.
- Over-reliance on written media (brochures, handouts, booklets).
- Inadequate briefing of local administrators.
- Talking down.
- Not enough relevant examples.
- Too much jargon in the brochure or in presentations.
- No opportunity to get queries answered.
- Slow feedback on choices made (individual statements).
- No communication plan for employees who join mid-year.
- Inconsistency of detail across the various media used.
- Poor-quality materials (remember, the medium is the message).

Communication is a key element in the flex plan process. Without considerable care in this area, the whole initiative risks being stillborn.

TAX, INSURANCE AND FINANCIAL PLANNING ISSUES

Although these issues will depend on the fiscal situation in each country, the principles remain constant. Because many financial benefits are age-related, in particular pensions, health and life assurance, employees doing the same job may not receive the same level of benefit. A 58-year-old man with heart problems will not be able to 'buy' the same amount of life cover for the same price as a 25-year-old amateur athlete. Older employees will have to spend more of their credits on such items, leaving fewer credits available to spend on more discretionary items, unless core benefits price this out.

In some schemes, pension contributions are included as a key part of a newly introduced flex plan to make the switch from an expensive pension benefit based on final salary to one based on money purchase. This is likely to be less onerous for the company in years to come. If the scheme offers a basic pension benefit for everyone with the flexibility to use other flex plan credits to top it up or use on other flexible benefits, those needing a high rate of pension funding could continue at the old level, with other employees choosing to fund their pension at a lower level.

In other schemes, pension contributions are totally excluded from the flex plan. It may be that the company has a high number of young employees who may not want to spend credits on pensions, or more simply, the company may wish to avoid the administration.

Although medical insurance take-up depends on the level of basic cover available from the state, many employees in the United Kingdom are taking on the responsibility of providing additional private health care to avoid the inevitable waiting times within government schemes and to be able to specify a specialist physician. But diagnostic costs are rising sharply, together with the corresponding monthly premiums. By providing private health care through a flex plan, employees can see the cost in 'credits' spent. Additional costs levied by the provider can be passed on to employees without reflecting badly on the company. The inevitable cross-subsidies between family members and single members will disappear. Employees pay only for their own level of benefit. The company is therefore no longer committed to having to budget for everyone to be covered at the expensive 'family grade' level. In terms of advantages to the company, this is one feature where companies break the link between open-ended commitment to benefit provision and the brave new world of 'defined cost'.

The benefits available under a flex plan are no different from those available under normal benefit schemes. The difference with a flex plan is the visibility of their cost to the employee. Once you have established a cost for each tranche of benefit, any increases in cost to the company or enhancements due to the employee's personal circumstances can be passed directly on to the employee in future years.

Pricing the flex plan

Pricing the flex plan is a complex task and not something to be taken on without some sound professional advice. There are several routes you could take, depending on your overriding reason for offering flexible benefits. Pricing is a sophisticated consultancy service which uses proven mathematical models to arrive at appropriate credit levels, but it depends what your objectives are.

- Provide employees with the same level of benefits as before, but with a wider element of choice.
- Reduce the level of benefits offered, but offset the change with a wider range.
- Subsidize older employee costs.
- Communicate the real cost of benefits to employees.
- Buy out old practices and expensive benefits.

Depending on your financial or strategic objectives, the cost of the flex plan will change according to which benefits you include at a standard threshold and which benefits you decide should be purchased on a credit-by-credit basis.

To offset the effects of unwise choices made by employees, you should always identify those benefits which may be subject to adverse selection prior to launch, and assess the likely impact on the overall costs and on the individuals concerned. If initial soundings suggest that the take-up may be adverse, you may need to impose some restrictions on choice or establish a minimum requirement for the advantage of all. But individual pricing helps, as does providing core benefits. You may decide to subsidize regular health checks to promote a healthier workforce, as this will in time feed back into lower insurance premiums.

Inevitably, there will be winners and losers in any newly formed flex plan. It is essential prior to any announcement that an estimate is made of the benefit/financial change within various subgroups to avoid wholesale rejection of the plan. Extreme cases (those whose benefits are reduced by 1 per cent or more) should be compensated in some other way. If possible avoid introducing the changes at the same time as the annual salary review, as 'losers' will compare their loss against their former salary and so feel more disadvantaged than they actually are.

The technique for costing the plan is one of modelling, testing, refitting and remodelling until such time as you are happy with the tolerance levels at the extremes. No scheme will work out perfectly, but with a series of checks and balances, using informed assumptions, you should be able to devise a flex plan to meet most people's perceptions.

ADMINISTRATION

Despite the obvious cost-control benefits to the employer and the freedom of choice flex plans offer to employees, many companies are put off at the implementation stage when they come to consider the administration aspects. But going beyond giving everyone the same benefits is bound to be more complex. You need to consider just how much more complex it will be to administer the new benefits.

The first task is to break down the administrative task into bite-sized chunks and apply some common sense. Flex plan administration systems are characterized by four key criteria:

- database format;
- employee selection procedures;
- links with other parts of the business;
- training of administrators.

Database format

Depending on the size and complexity of the scheme, you can choose to set up a manual system, a spreadsheet system, a system integrated with the existing personnel/payroll system or an independent flex plan system. No system is intrinsically better than any other. Your choice depends on what the system will be required to deliver and the funds that are available to pay for it.

You need to consider the IT requirements:

- number of participants;
- range of benefit options;
- frequency of amending choices;
- location of staff;
- existing in-house IT resources, links to other internal systems;
- complexity of the pricing system;
- IT awareness among staff;
- level of database analysis required;
- costs, both for the initial outlay and the maintenance costs.

There are several proprietary software packages available on the market, normally through your flex plan consultant, which will encompass many of the above parameters. An example of such a system is the Flexible Benefits Module developed by employee benefits software specialist Motivano. It is a PC-based package which can also be used for non-flex plans as a benefits management system. It can operate independently or interface with existing human resources systems, and can export data or merge with in-house systems such as word processing or desk-top publishing packages. The key functions include:

- employee data maintenance;
- calculation of credits per employee;
- selection of benefits by employee;
- reports (additions, deletions, cost centre, P11D).

Whichever system you choose, the package should be able to administrate the selection of benefits (and the amount of individual benefit) by employees and report on those selections. The selection process should include an enquiry system so that employees can try out various permutations before deciding on specific choices. Once a selection has been made there should be a personal illustration of the impact of the choices made, in the form of a rewards or benefits statement and the new benefit levels chosen, with any appropriate caveats about an unbalanced selection. The system should also indicate when the benefits will commence. Some may be immediate, at the end of the month, or at some future date. In all cases the selection should trigger any relevant changes to payroll and the statutory requirements for employment law reporting.

Employee selection procedures

It is important with any new internal system that you take time to make the system as user-friendly as possible, especially with a subject as little understood as benefits. The project team needs to decide what would be the best way for employees to make their selections. If the procedure is too complicated, employees will fail to take advantage of flex and you will have incurred considerable consultancy cost for nothing. If the workforce is mature, working in a traditional industrial environment, you may find that manual input on paper is the most attractive way to get participation, although it may be the least efficient. If the workforce is IT-friendly and used to functioning through a networked PC system, on-screen benefit selection is an obvious route.

You should take care not to lose the human touch. There should always be an opportunity for employees to talk to the designated flex administrator about the choices available before confirming the selection. Not only does it provide reassurance, it can be a useful way for those familiar with the system to pick up any employee difficulties or misconceptions about the flex plan that may have come about through rumour, misinformation or simply poor communication.

Linking flex plans into the business

Because 30 per cent or more of the company's total overhead could be benefits-related, you need to ensure that, whichever system you adopt, the system is compatible with all the associated systems to do with employee costs. There will be reporting implications across a wide spectrum: National Insurance, tax, payroll, statutory reporting and general overheads budget. Because a flex plan involves individuals making personal choices, the final management of the allocation of benefits will be much more complex than before. The full implication of the new reporting requirements needs to be examined carefully so that all the loose ends are picked up and pigeon-holed.

Training

Training of the main administrators is crucial, but not just in file maintenance. The site or divisional administrator of the new flex plan will be the representative of all that is good about individual choice of benefits. The flex plan administrator should therefore be articulate about the theory as well as the practice, and be an enthusiastic ambassador for the scheme, either on a one-to-one basis or as part of a project team. The administrator should also be experienced enough to anticipate any systems problems when it comes to interfacing with other company-wide packages and report them appropriately so that errors or malfunctions are not ignored.

Running through all four criteria is the link with your benefit providers. All providers need to be consulted in the development of your delivery systems so that the employees are well served.

IS CHOICE OF BENEFITS MOTIVATIONAL?

There is no doubt that for many organizations, flexible benefits plans provide a way to be more responsive to the individual's need to take more direct control over benefits due to changing lifestyles. But what part does a flex plan play in the quest for performance improvement?

'Flexing' is still in its early days, even in developed countries with the possible exception of the United States. The advantages to both employee and employer have been outlined in this chapter. Because there are relatively few examples of schemes up and running, unequivocal proof that retention can be increased, recruitment costs can be lessened and cost control can be improved are at present anecdotal by the standards of science. But if you are using flexible benefits as part of a general company strategy to unlock the potential of individuals to improve their effectiveness at work by making their remuneration more appropriate, the moral argument has been won.

Whether flexible benefits, as the plans mature, can be used as tactical incentive devices to focus attention on key business issues such as higher key task performance has yet to be tested. There are many situations where offering additional flex plan credits to reward desirable behaviour seems like a perfect method to tie performance to reward in a personally relevant way.

In short, flex plans form part of the motivational jigsaw which, if integrated into a performance improvement culture for non-sales staff, could be one of the major driving forces towards higher efficiency. By themselves, at the very least they allow you to control your costs better and offer employees more choice over how they are remunerated. If fully integrated, a flex plan could be the catalyst to a workforce transformed by the freedom of personal choice in how they are paid to improve performance at work in a tangible way. That has to be a better way to retain employees or recruit new ones in the future.

SUMMARY

- Benefits provide a way to offer staff basic economic security.
- They become a means to attract and retain staff.
- By offering the choice of how much to take of which benefit, a company can be shown to be more responsive.
- Administration and communication are crucial to the sound introduction of flexible benefits.
- It is still early days to assess the effect of flex plans, but anecdotal evidence suggests they can increase retention and recruiting competitiveness.

7 | Incentive travel: everyone's top reward

Holidays are an expensive trial of strength. The only satisfaction comes from survival.

Jonathan Miller

EXTRAORDINARY REWARDS

After considering cash and benefits as incentives and finding both wanting as motivational tools in isolation, we are left with a myriad of non-cash options to choose from. But of all the possible non-cash rewards you could offer as part of a motivation programme, a travel experience is by far the most popular. It is also the most expensive. Depending on where you go and what you do, you could be spending anywhere between £500 and £5,000 per person. If you consider that professional incentive travel always includes a partner (husband, wife, boyfriend or girl-friend), qualifiers need to have achieved exceptional levels of performance, simply to make the whole thing pay for itself. It also requires an extraordinary level of logistical planning.

But extraordinary is what incentive travel is all about. Incentive travel is not just an expensive package holiday. There are many tour operators who can supply that product. There are significant features which differentiate incentive travel from promotional or holiday travel. The main difference is that participants normally travel as a group rather than as individuals, although in the United States travel rewards for individuals and their families are often included in incentive travel statistics. But travelling as a group is not the only difference.

A definition may help. This one was compiled by the ITMA (Incentive Travel & Meetings Association) in the United Kingdom.

> Incentive travel is that discipline of sales and marketing and management which uses promise, fulfilment and memory of an exceptional travel related experience to motivate participating individuals to attain exceptional levels of achievement in their places of work or education.

It comes as a surprise to many potential clients that incentive travel is in fact a marketing technique. Like any other marketing technique it needs to be appropriate, budgeted for and managed effectively.

Incentive travel is by far the most popular reward within the framework of an integrated motivation programme, after cash. But the reasons for this are not simply because travel is expensive and therefore highly valued as a reward. Travel sits right at the heart of effective motivation for all kinds of psychological reasons. It appeals to all the senses. It offers relaxation from a stressful life. It has 'trophy value': you can impress the neighbours by talking about where you are going and where you have been. Peer group pressure to qualify with your high-achieving colleagues is very strong within a commercial environment. High achievers like to be formally recognized for a job well done and to meet influential senior management. There is team member pressure to 'join the club' and become one of the elite. It is also a powerful sales management tool in retaining top achievers until some time after the end of their effort to qualify.

It is no accident that most 12-month programmes do not fulfil the reward promise until three or four months after the end of the qualification period. This is not only to ensure enough time to make the necessary arrangements. By the time the incentive event is over, based on the previous year's performance, the top achievers are three or four months into the next cycle of qualification and probably already leading the pack. It is difficult to ignore the anticipation of another complimentary long-haul holiday for the sake of a new employer with new products to learn about and no guarantee of repeating success. So people who attend incentive travel events tend to be retained longer than those who do not regularly qualify. But does it work?

AEG: off to the orient

AEG, the German white goods manufacturer with subsidiaries in the major European countries, ran a four-month campaign aimed at key stockists called 'Off to the Orient'. It had analysed the contribution from its 800 stockists and discovered there were only 200 serious business partners. The rest were occasional trade purchasers. Of the 200 established stockists, the top 40 (20 per cent) produced 80 per cent of the business.

By leaguing stockists into eight turnover bands, AEG was able to offer a guaranteed trip to Hong Kong for the top five in each league. The number of participants in each league differed depending on the size of the stockist's historic purchases. The big providers had a one-in-two chance of qualifying. The smaller providers had a progressively lower chance. In this way AEG was able to satisfy its major stockists and provide a keen element of competition for the rest.

A fast-start award of a weekend in Amsterdam was offered for everyone who achieved target over the first two months of the campaign. Sales people in the retail outlets could win a series of Chinese-style merchandise awards by picking out a lucky Chinese fortune stick when the field representative called, provided the sales person had sold an AEG machine during that cycle. The results were impressive. Many of the top stockists increased their purchases by 20 per cent, some by as much as 50 per cent. AEG also benefited from the fast-start mechanism by unprecedented levels of immediate sales in a traditionally average-to-slow retail sales period.

Gaggenau: sophisticated refrigeration

Gaggenau retailers and designers were offered the opportunity to attend a hosted event in Sweden, staying at the famous Ice Hotel, by selling specialist refrigeration units over an eight-month period. The 50 winning participants enjoyed a varied programme of dog-sledding, snowmobile excursions, ice fishing, Lapp cuisine, and open-air barbecues, set up in a traditional Sami teepee. The unusual nature of the travel experience produced a growth in sales of some 50 per cent, based on the same period the previous year.

PROMISING THE EARTH

What is meant by 'promise' in the definition of incentive travel? In product terms the destination needs to be sold to the participants *before* they start to compete rather than after the race is over. It is an incentive to promote higher performance, not a reward for achieving whatever would have been achieved anyway. It also has to be recognized that if planned correctly and because of the per head costs, fewer than 20 per cent of the programme participants will qualify for the incentive trip, so the power of the incentive for most of the participants lies in the anticipation rather than the fulfilment.

The choice of incentive destination starts with what possibilities there may be to promote the venue, even though the majority of participants may never have been there and may never qualify. It follows that not every place in the world can be a universally popular incentive destination. Cities like London, Paris or New York are bona fide world players as far as the image of the destination is concerned. They need little explanation and offer a wide range of attractive features to many levels of participant in many cultures. Other places may in reality be equally fascinating but will need to be promoted in much the same way as any local tourist office would present any location. Evian, on the shores of Lake Geneva, for example is not well known beyond France and Switzerland, but can provide everything necessary for a top-class incentive event. Depending on your perspective, some cold and windy destinations in northern Europe are irresistible to people who live in hot climates, simply because they represent an alternative lifestyle.

It is often said that the best way to promote a destination is to take people there so they can experience it for themselves. This explains why the consumer travel industry spends so much time hosting even the most junior retail travel clerks off peak to their latest destinations at what seems great expense. It is the only way to get the distributors to know the product. However, with incentive travel, the participants cannot attend the event first and qualify later. For that reason, a clear and objective assessment of how the destination is likely to be perceived has to be made. Paris may be old hat to an experienced group, but to first timers it cannot be beaten. In fact statistically the majority of first-time incentive groups out of the United Kingdom visit Paris.

Perception is everything

So the motivational power of a destination is concerned more with perception than reality. In other words, for the particular group you wish to motivate the question is whether London/Paris/New York is going to give you the right cluster of perceptions you need to achieve maximum motivation, given the available budget. A recent poll of European meeting planners rated the appeal of conference destinations around the world. Top was Paris, bottom was Glasgow. But in between there were some obvious perceptions and some less obvious misperceptions. (See Table 7.1.)

The top 20 could serve equally well as a list of popular incentive travel destinations, apart from perhaps Geneva which has a more business-like image commensurate with what conference organizers are looking for. Some destinations do not deserve to be perceived so poorly. Dubai at next to bottom was just starting to make itself known to the incentive travel market at the time of the survey, but offers exceptional incentive travel features to experienced buyers. As with any market, fashions change. In the

Table 7.1 Appeal of conference destinations

Destination	Average score	Destination	Average score
Paris	8.0	Los Angeles	6.4
Hawaii	7.8	Lisbon	6.4
Hong Kong	7.5	Budapest	6.3
Singapore	7.5	Brussels	6.3
New York	7.5	Edinburgh	6.2
Geneva	7.4	Copenhagen	6.1
London	7.4	Milan	5.9
Cannes	7.3	Stockholm	5.9
Monaco	7.3	Istanbul	5.8
Rome	7.1	Cyprus	5.8
Florence	7.1	Munich	5.8
Nice	7.1	Frankfurt	5.7
Vienna	7.0	Athens	5.6
Amsterdam	6.9	Dublin	5.6
Bangkok	6.8	Luxembourg	5.3
Barcelona	6.7	Marbella	5.3
Berlin	6.7	Helsinki	5.2
Madrid	6.4	Cairo	4.9
Miami	6.4	Dubai	4.3
Zurich	6.4	Glasgow	4.2

Source: Reed International.

late 1980s Athens was a popular European incentive destination, combining culture and beach life in a unique way. Through the 1990s, it lost its appeal because of publicity about poor airport safety and the genuinely high levels of pollution in downtown Athens, although a recent ban on private cars and investment in the city's transport systems in readiness for the 2004 Olympics much improved this situation.

Many trade magazines carry annual incentive travel destination surveys, and these are as much a reflection of the economy or advertising as they are the attractiveness of the destination in absolute terms. Table 7.2 gives the results of a survey carried out in 2004 for destinations ex-UK by a leading magazine, *Meetings & Incentive Travel*.

Table 7.2 Long-haul and short-haul outbound UK incentive destinations

Long haul		Short haul	
1.	Cape Town	1.	Paris
2.	New York	2.	Barcelona
3.	Mauritius	3.	Madrid
4.	Bangkok	4.	Seville
5.	Miami	5.	Prague
6.	Las Vegas	6.	Marbella
7.	Dubai	7.	Disneyland Paris
8.	Orlando	8.	Vienna
9.	Chicago	9.	Tenerife
10.	New Orleans	10.	Rome

Source: *Meetings & Incentive Travel*, June 2004.

It is interesting to note that of the top 10 long-haul destinations, six are to the United States, and in the short-haul table, four are to Spain. This trend is therefore somewhat reliant on good, value for money air flights with schedules to suit the incentive groups market.

The important point for the incentive travel organizer is to keep in touch with the perceptions of the average participant. If the destination is too obscure or snobbish you will lose impact, particularly if you have to labour to explain its attractions. Aspen, Colorado, has been hitting the headlines in recent years, not least because of the patronage of the British royal family and senior members of the US administration. As such it has acquired a higher profile as an incentive destination than it would other-wise. Scottsdale, Arizona has been very well sold to the incentives industry in the United Kingdom and hence comes up quite often as a viable US alternative to Las Vegas or San Francisco. But it needs to be sold hard even to experienced buyers, whose partic-ipants will probably have no immediate perception of what Scottsdale can offer. Destinations need to be promoted vigor-ously in order to gain acceptance.

Iveco go to nepal

Logic does not always rule the day. Iveco-France (truck manufac-turers) ran a highly successful travel incentive programme built around the creative concept of climbing mountains. Called 'Vaincre' (to conquer), it invited truck dealers to compete over three three-month stages through a sales product quiz and the appropriate usage of supplied promotional material. The top 30 qualified for a selection of aspirational merchandise or a luxuri-ous weekend away. The next 10 won a sporting weekend in Chamonix (Mont Blanc). The top five would form an accompa-nied incentive travel trip to Nepal including a visit to the foothills of Mount Everest. Full creative licence was given to the promo-tion of the campaign, including flags to stick on a wallchart, a video about Everest, individual performance bulletins, postcards from the destination and 'expedition notebooks' to record mar-keting activities completed to date. It worked. Iveco raised its market share by four percentage points to 22.5 per cent over the nine-month programme period.

Easy access

Destination appeal is also about accessibility. If you cannot get there in one flight, the potential qualifiers will not find the des-tination so attractive. Around the world there are some stun-ning hotel properties, but lack of international air access is a constant logistical stumbling block to being able to use some properties on a consistent basis for groups. Cyprus, for exam-ple, has several world-class hotels but access is restricted by a relatively small number of scheduled air services from European countries. Although the hotels can deliver the num-ber of luxury rooms required and superb leisure facilities, get-ting there is less easy than getting to Vienna, for example, particularly from northern Europe, which represents the island's main market. Madeira is another destination with great appeal to certain sections of the European market, but it requires at least one change of plane for most visitors on scheduled flights.

As companies become more security conscious and ask for split flights, so that the risk of losing all their top people on one flight is reduced should there be a plane crash, satisfying the requirement to get everyone to the destination on the same day in time for the inaugural dinner could be a tall order. Getting them all there within 12 hours is fine. To do it within three hours is often impossible.

Promoting the image

To present the promise, you need to promote what is on offer. Incentive travel only exists in the participants' minds until they qualify for the trip. The image of the destination needs to be carefully promoted in the same way that any product would be. Promotion can range from a video, CD-Rom or wallposter through to a brochure, a local artefact, a postcard from the destination, e-mail messages, a website or even an advertisement in the newspaper local to the destination, hoping to welcome company qualifiers next spring! Whatever is decided, there should be a plan to keep the destination high on the agenda of those who could qualify. This is particularly important in the middle stages of the qualification period when interest and enthusiasm are likely to be sagging. Because the budgets for incentive travel are high compared with other sales promotion projects, you need to make the most of your investment. For that reason qualification periods can be anything up to two years. The usual period is 12 calendar months, closely tied into the financial year so that qualification at the year end is related to the overall business performance of individuals against their peers.

A promotional plan needs to be drawn up, budgeted for and adhered to, if you are going to achieve your incremental performance objectives. Many programmes suffer from a 'launch it and leave it' attitude, where all the promotion happens at the beginning of the programme and there are no coherent messages during the campaign. If you choose a destination with positive perceptions you should have a lot to say during the qualification period to encourage participants to focus their efforts on achieving higher performance.

A typical incentive travel promotion plan would be high on gloss, competition detail, qualifiers' names and photos, with specific timings about the itinerary left until nearer the end of the qualifying period. It is tempting to think that if you can promote the destination well enough, the event will take care of itself. The incentive travel experience must go beyond expectations to the point that the event becomes the best advertisement to requalify for the following year. There is nothing more dispiriting than a product which does not at the very least meet expectations, especially if you have made an extraordinary personal effort to qualify.

TYPICAL INCENTIVE TRAVEL PROMOTION SCHEDULE

Oct–Dec	Development, costing, design of materials.
January	Launch at a sales conference. Brochure, video, monthly competition bulletin.
March	Teaser from the destination. Newsletter promoting hotel.
June	Teaser, mid-year results. Newsletter promoting destination. Video to support destination message.
October	Teaser, 'Fast Finish double points' promotion, newsletter promoting pro rata qualifiers. Draft itinerary.
January	Final results, congratulations bulletin, joining instructions for qualifiers. (Launch of next year's programme.)

BT using the internet to promote colorado

To increase revenue through British Telecom's Corporate Clients channel, promotion and communication about an incentives programme were effected via BT's own intranet and a website dedicated to the campaign. Participants could find out about the programme via their electronic systems, and were able to check their latest position in the league tables online. Various promotion bulletins were issued on the intranet, regarding the top event in Colorado and Arizona. Lower tiers were rewarded with retail vouchers that could be redeemed via a screen-based redemption process. The campaign produced revenue growth through this channel of 300 per cent, providing a return of 250:1 on the original promotional investment.

MAKING INCENTIVE TRAVEL DIFFERENT

As a product, incentive travel is very different from an upmarket package holiday, even though the hotel and destination may well be the same. This is not only because you travel as part of a group. It is all about enhancing the travel experience. The group nature of incentive travel means that enhancements can be made to the travel experience that are not normally available to the individual holidaymaker, without considerable organization and expense.

Off-airport check-in

At the airport of departure, you can arrange for qualifiers' luggage to be checked in at a nearby hotel so that they do not have to queue up with everyone else at the terminal. Airlines at busy airports often prefer to operate in this way as it means less administration at the terminal check-in desk and less crowding in the departure hall with large groups.

The advantages for the organizer are what makes incentive travel different. Qualifiers feel they have been singled out for special treatment. They are transferred to the terminal together as a group, so there is no possibility of them getting lost. They can begin to socialize with other members of the group. This 'getting to know each other' process is an important element of what incentive travel offers. If the group can establish an early common bond, they tend to enjoy the experience much more. As many groups will be from the same company or industry, they will already know more about each other's lifestyle than most holiday-making individuals meeting for the first time. They can relax about the ticketing and travel arrangements as they know this is being handled by the professional group organizer. From the participants' angle, the administrative detail involved in international travel is largely taken care of.

We used to handle an annual convention for a very large IT company. Each year we would take 300–400 senior managers and sales people to a European destination for four or five nights, staying at a top-class hotel. Part of the post-event research process was to interview at random some of the participants to establish any improvements we could make for the following year. I sat in on a few of the sessions with the researchers. When asked a general question about the appeal of incentive travel to top achievers, the local manager said, 'You know, I spend most of my working day taking difficult decisions, dealing with people problems, worrying about the market and planning for an uncertain and unpredictable future. As soon as I check in for the convention (annual incentive travel event), I know I can take my brain out of gear and not have to think or plan or worry – just enjoy myself. It's only for a week or so each year, but I really do look forward to being organized by someone else for a change.'

From the organizers' viewpoint an off-airport check-in also means they know who has checked in before the departure to the airport, and so can take contingency action for named and identified latecomers or no-shows. If the qualifiers have been invited to stay overnight the day before departure (an early-morning check-in may be necessary), they have an opportunity to get to know their fellow qualifiers and the company hosts. The organizers can make any announcements, introduce themselves and their role, and double-check any last-minute queries, particularly to do with passports or the return itinerary.

If the destination requires entry visas, the incentive travel organizer will normally organize the administrative detail and pay any fees due, for later reimbursement from the sponsoring company.

Enhancing the journey

Incentive travel includes negotiating the best possible deal on the aircraft, but not just the price. Special needs such as aisle seats, window seats, more leg room, special diets or non-smoking can be requested long before the group checks in. This means that qualifiers can enjoy a more comfortable journey than simply taking pot-luck at the check-in desk, or worse still, being bumped off the flight because of over-booking by the carrier.

If the flight is chartered for the exclusive use of the group at a specific departure time, personalized headrests, meals, particular drinks and even particular video entertainment can be arranged. One group of automotive dealers who were due to be going home on a long-haul flight were bemoaning the fact that because of the gala dinner the night before travelling, they would miss a world championship boxing match. We recorded the fight on video in the hotel during the gala dinner and after the evening meal on board the overnight charter the next day, we ran the video of the previous night's boxing. The qualifiers were overwhelming in their gratitude. The idea to do it was priceless, but it cost the client no more than the price of a blank videotape.

More travellers does not always mean less cost

One common misconception among incentive travel buyers is that the more people you book on a flight, the lower the price. With most other commodities, there would be a discount for bulk purchase. There is always a group rate which is lower than the published fare, but greater numbers does not automatically lead to a further reduction in price. An airline seat has a finite life. There are only so many seats on one aircraft flying from one destination to another. When the airline works out its yield – how much revenue it needs on that particular flight to make a profit – it knows a certain proportion of the market will buy a certain number of seats at a specific price: first class, business, economy or wait-listed. It is not unusual for one transatlantic airliner to be carrying passengers who paid 25 or more different prices to go from London to New York on the same flight.

Although incentive group fares are negotiated through the special groups department and will normally be cheaper than published scheduled fares, how much cheaper depends on the availability of seats at that cheaper price. (Airlines know a guaranteed number of business seats will be sold in the last few days before departure from their bookings history database.) It may be that on the scheduled flight you have identified as being perfect for your group, the airline will only allow you to take 40 seats at the discounted rate, because it knows it can sell the balance at a higher price. So you either pay the higher price, split the flight with another carrier, or cost out a charter for the whole group.

Buying airline space is one of the great black arts of incentive travel. Very often it is not what you know, but who the organizer knows within the airline which can secure the best deal for the client.

Charter options

One option is to charter an aircraft. An entire library could be produced on the intricacies of airplane charters, but as far as incentive travel is concerned the relevant factors are:

- number of travellers (pax);
- budget;
- accessibility of destination.

You may find you are unable to buy enough seats at the price you want using scheduled services. There may not be a convenient departure time for eventual arrival at the destination. In the case of an island or remote venue, there may not be a scheduled flight on the day you want.

Chartering is an alternative option. You pay a fixed price for the plane based on fuel costs, so you need to find a plane which most nearly suits the size of your group to get the best value cost per head. Because it is most unlikely you will be bringing qualifiers back home the moment they arrive at the destination, you will usually pay for the 'empty leg'. Occasionally, the charter company may have another client with similar numbers who could take up the empty leg. But this is unlikely, unless it is a series of charters, as would happen during the holiday season for a tour operator, so the cost of fuel for the return flight has to be factored in. In general, chartering is an expensive option. Availability of a suitable aircraft may not be confirmed until a few weeks before departure, such is the nature of the *ad hoc* charter market. Some corporate clients find this an unacceptable arrangement, as it always carries the risk that no suitable plane can be found within the available budget, leaving qualifiers stranded at the airport.

The destination decision may well depend on flight accessibility, so careful thought needs to be given to the practical question of whether the qualifiers can actually get there comfortably and at the right price.

Baggage

One of the banes of international travel when you travel as an individual is baggage. Incentive travel is about treating the qualifiers as VIP guests and smoothing their passage through the unavoidable procedures of travelling. A professional incentive travel organizer, as mentioned above, will arrange for baggage to be checked in at an off-airport hotel so that qualifiers can go straight through customs. At the destination, baggage has to be personally identified in the normal way in the baggage hall, but the incentive group organizer can often arrange for porters to come 'airside' to take the baggage away if permitted and deliver it to the hotel by special baggage vans. If this is done, the baggage can get to the hotel before the qualifiers, enabling it to be delivered to rooms in time for the qualifiers' arrival, if logistics allow. So there is no struggling with suitcases from customs to the taxi rank and then wondering on arrival at the hotel how long the porters will take delivering them to your room.

Hotel check-in

Checking in at a hotel is often cited in research as being something guests consider a necessary evil. The proliferation of 'preferred guest' schemes for frequent business travellers offering instant check-in facilities in the form of a pre-prepared guest envelope similar to the system used by car-hire firms is one way to combat this. Incentive groups already benefit from this system. The group organizer will have sent a rooming list to the hotel some days before departure. While the group is in the air, the hotel will be allocating names to rooms. Sometimes, if the hotel is at low capacity, the rooming allocation can even be done the day before the group travels, providing the opportunity for the organizer to write the actual room numbers on the baggage tags as they are checked in prior to departure. This speeds up the porterage considerably at the destination, especially if the organizer has promised a better than average tip for prompt delivery of the group's bags.

It is a source of constant wonder around the world how adept hotel porters can be at recognizing items of baggage at a glance by noting mentally some feature of the baggage with the personality of the owner. However, I remember one occasion when we managed to do completely the wrong thing (see the Volvo case history in Chapter 1). We had organized a three-month incentive campaign with the top qualifiers travelling to Venice on the Orient Express. Part of the incentive programme was a 'fast start' award of a set of Orient Express baggage for anyone who achieved 100 per cent of their first month's target. Unfortunately they all did!

The result was that everyone who qualified for the trip had identical Orient Express luggage. If you have ever arrived in Venice by train, you will know that the baggage is piled up in a big heap at the end of the platform on disembarkation and you simply claim your suitcase from the baggage mound. Fortunately for the qualifiers it was our job to transfer the baggage, so we were the ones who had to wade through 50 identical sets of luggage and allocate each of them to the relevant qualifier's room. Clearly the organizer can never be too prepared and should always be ready for unexpected eventualities.

Saving time

On arrival at the hotel (the baggage having been delivered earlier by separate transport), qualifiers should be able to pick up their keys and hotel information at a check-in desk, separate from the main hotel reception desk, often manned by client company staff. This provides a friendly and trouble-free welcome without any potential language difficulties or delays. Often on arrival a cocktail party will be organized in a private part of the hotel to allow a little more time for baggage to be delivered to rooms, for the hosts to make a brief welcome speech, and for qualifiers to relax and take in their new surroundings.

It used to be the done thing to personalize the hotel, so that when the group arrived there was something familiar to see. Typically the hotel lobby would carry company logo banners or there would be a local band playing welcome songs behind a huge company flag. On one occasion I put a group into a beach resort where all the rooms had balconies overlooking a spectacularly wide pool, not visible from the lobby area. We took the decision not to put up big banners and logos, as the group felt they did not want to be identified as being part of a convention. They were an upmarket, sophisticated crowd. But the organizer asked us to do something to acknowledge that the group had arrived. So when the qualifiers walked out on to their balconies for the first time to admire the view, they would naturally look down on the pool area. In the middle of the pool we had constructed the company logo in flowers and floated them on the pool surface as a welcome gesture.

Dinearounds

For some people a daunting aspect of foreign travel is where to eat outside the hotel. As part of an incentive group, eating out in professionally vetted restaurants with local atmosphere becomes a pleasure rather than a trial. Dinearound events are set up, and three or four high-quality restaurants are chosen. Qualifiers can choose which restaurant they prefer from supplied prospectuses on the welcome desk. Often they will arrange to go with a group of other qualifiers, sit at the same table and make an evening of it. Company executives will be instrumental in making everyone feel involved, and hosts can make new qualifiers feel welcome by inviting them to 'their' restaurant to introduce them to other qualifiers. No one is left on their own, unless they want to be.

Special excursions and activities

Every incentive destination will afford opportunities to do some sightseeing. By their very nature, there will be places any tourist could visit. But incentive travel organizers will work with local ground agents to ensure that if there is a chance to do or see something not normally available to the tourist, they will arrange it.

In terms of a venue for dinner it could be a government building in Eastern Europe, a private chateau in the Loire Valley, an exclusive art gallery in Athens or a film star's home in California. Instead of a bus tour, individual transport with or without chauffeur can be organized, with perhaps a few off-the-beaten track places to visit pointed out.

For example, a jeep or mini-moke safari in Barbados is a relaxed way to explore this relatively small Caribbean island. Qualifiers are each assigned an open-top jeep and a sealed envelope containing questions about the history or culture of the island. With careful planning, the questions can be framed so as to ensure a three or four-hour round trip, ending up at a specific restaurant for a group lunch. Qualifiers can operate independently or split up into teams to encourage a competitive edge. For more enterprising groups, cryptic clues can be set which may involve questioning local inhabitants on things only a local would know.

In some parts of the world it is possible to farm small groups out to spend an evening with a local family to see how the local people really live. This provides some fascinating insights into a country you may only ever visit once in your life. It also allows some money to go back into the local economy, other than through the cash registers at the hotel bar.

SOME UNUSUAL INCENTIVE TRAVEL ACTIVITIES

- Dinner in a tent near Muscat.
- Whale hunting off Vancouver.
- Private charter of US presidential yacht.
- Helicopter landing on the deck of an aircraft carrier.
- Breakfast on the banks of the Zambezi.

- Vintage car rally.
- Lunch on the Great Wall of China.
- 'Jailhouse Rock' party on Alcatraz.
- Police bike escort in New Orleans from airport to hotel.
- Murder Mystery on the Orient Express.
- A real diamond in your cocktail in Amsterdam.
- Dragon-boat racing in Hong Kong.
- Playing soccer with Pele.
- Towel party in a Turkish bath.
- Attacked by Saracens in the Jordanian desert.
- Dinner with the Inuit in an igloo.
- Sailing a 19th-century square-rigger.

The range of bespoke activities for incentive groups is restricted only by the imagination of the organizer and the budget of the sponsoring company.

The conference session

It used to be fashionable to pretend there would be a conference session during the overseas event, in the mistaken belief that the event could be written off against company tax. It was also hoped that individual qualifiers could avoid personal tax if the event was promoted as a business conference or seminar rather than a competition prize.

Tax regimes vary and are currently in a state of flux around the world regarding incentive travel. However, in the United States, most of Europe and Australia, all incentive travel events based on competitive qualification are taxable as benefits to the participant and, in some cases, his or her partner. Legislation and enforcement has become much tighter in recent years, with some major corporations having to dig deep into reserves to pay tax liabilities stretching back several years, following an investigation by the tax authorities.

The result has been a decrease in the number of incentive travel clients that run a conference session, now that there is no fiscal advantage. It is an opportunity wasted. The conference session, however short, allows the company to recognize publicly its top achievers, encourages active participation in corporate aims from the partners and binds the group together. Cottrell in 'Social facilitation' (1972)[1] studied the specific effect of the mere presence of others on individual performance. He concluded that when two or more act together, the intensity of their individual behaviour often increases. Individual goal setting and motivation can be vastly improved by insisting on a conference session, even though there may be little on the agenda which is serious business information.

Partners should be included so that more understanding of the company partners' contribution to the corporation's aims is possible. It also reinforces the virtuous cycle of achievement/recognition/support/achievement.

Gala dinner

The night before departing for home, the incentive organizer will normally be required to arrange the gala dinner. This is an opportunity to pull all the qualifiers and their partners together, make a few speeches, perhaps present awards to top achievers, take some photographs and consolidate all the special treatment the qualifiers have enjoyed during the previous few days. Often, because of the large numbers involved, a private cabaret and band can be organized for relatively low cost per person. Each group will respond differently, so careful thought must be given to what would be appropriate. The possibilities range from a local after-dinner speaker to an internationally known pop group. But, whoever is chosen, the staging implication needs to be thought through. Sound and lighting equipment could cost more than the cabaret fee in some countries, particularly if the audience is a large one.

One year we organized a gala dinner around the pool of the Astir Palace Hotel, on the Greek coast near Athens. But there was not enough floor space to accommodate the cabaret artiste and her band who were flown in especially. The only solution was to build a staging platform over part of the pool. With the judicious use of coloured theatrical lighting and the existing pool illumination, it proved to be a spectacular gala dinner showpiece which will stay in the memories of those who participated for many years to come.

Extended stays

One of the hidden advantages of qualifying for an incentive travel trip as a participant is free air transport to and from the destination. This leads inevitably to the opportunity to extend the length of time a qualifier could stay in the destination, or indeed travel on from there to another destination before returning home. This is particularly attractive on long-haul incentives where the expense and travelling effort have already taken place. Open-jaw air tickets – where qualifiers can enter a country through one airport and exit through a different airport in the same country at no extra cost – enable add-ons to be a highly economic way to enhance the reward.

It is not unusual for the incentive organizer to offer extended stays for a small administrative fee, often with a choice of three or four extension packages. Sometimes, an individual itinerary can be organized outside specific add-on packages, but this can be expensive if it involves forfeiting the group return air fare because some participants are returning from a different part of the world or country.

Extended stays can be an incentive in themselves. Qualifiers with relatives in Australia may consider an incentive to the Far East as part-funding to visit their Australian family, and as such it will have a powerful influence on work rate and performance, especially if the partner is pushing the participant to qualify.

Making incentive travel special

Throughout an incentive travel event there will be opportunities to enhance the experience for qualifiers, depending on the available budget. A visit to a vineyard could be made special by giving a free bottle of wine. A tour of a cathedral could be enhanced by a complimentary copy of the glossy booklet in the appropriate language and an expert guide. The traditional turn-down of the bed-covers at a hotel could be accompanied by a small gift of local origin as a surprise for qualifiers who may have been out all day following their own itinerary. It has become almost obligatory to provide a partner's gift to be placed at their place at the gala dinner, even if none of these other enhancements are made.

The guiding principle is to do as much as possible to ensure that the qualifiers are made to feel special, particularly their partners, who may have had to make many personal sacrifices during the year in order that the potential qualifier could reach the required standard. The budget is less important than the investment in the future morale of that qualifier to continue to achieve those standards within the framework of the sponsoring company.

Making the memory last

Most companies that use incentive travel for promoting performance improvement stress the effectiveness of marketing the event to those who did not qualify as well as those who did. If incentive travel is being used as a medium-term technique – not just for one isolated campaign – you should invest in providing memories of the event. As we know from personal experience, holiday memories as well as suntans fade rapidly once you are back at work. It is vital to keep that memory alive to encourage the continuation of those improved levels of performance for the subsequent year.

A photo album is one way to keep the memories fresh. A photographer could be engaged to cover the entire event or specific activities in the programme. An album would then be presented to each qualifier at the end as a souvenir. A less expensive variation is a gala dinner individual, table or group photograph presented in a stylish frame with the destination name and year of qualification. For those who did not qualify, the photographs can be turned into a glossy magazine with testimonials from the qualifiers to help promote the following year's destination.

Increasingly, video records are being kept so that the sounds as well as the sights can be captured. Video is much more powerful than print at a conference or launch event in helping to communicate the atmosphere and cameo of the event to those who did not attend. Video, CD copies or access to the post-event website will ensure that non-qualifying colleagues will get to see what went on and, we hope, encourage those colleagues to qualify during the following year. The objective of the images would be to recognize publicly as many qualifiers as possible rather than be an amateur travelogue, so careful editing is required to ensure every qualifier and partner is shown.

TRENDS IN INCENTIVE TRAVEL

According to some market surveys, global incentive travel is here to stay, and in general is growing faster than the economies in which it is used. But any predictions or trends need to be viewed in the context of the particular outbound market. Usage of incentive travel as a technique is a function of the development of the economy, population and geographical location. Not everyone goes to the same destination in the same numbers from the same places. Certainly within Europe, destination trends depend as much on who your neighbour is and your colonial heritage as the objective appeal of the destination.

Recently and particularly since the terrorist attacks of 9/11 the use of incentive travel has slowed. Some European clients have even taken policy decisions not to travel to the United States or on US carriers, simply to minimize the risk of being targeted by extremists. However, there are many areas of the world that are subject to changing political trends, such as the Middle East, Indonesia and Africa, and as such will require careful assessment of the risks versus the promotional value of going somewhere unusual or off the beaten track.

Within Europe there is a trend to go to the nearest neighbour first, then somewhere culturally opposite (Italy to Germany, Portugal to the United Kingdom; see Table 7.3). Beyond Europe,

Table 7.3 Where do Europeans go?

Country	First market	%	Second market	%
Belgium	Netherlands	43	Germany	15
Denmark	Germany	36	Sweden	21
Germany	Netherlands	18	United States	13
Greece	Germany	24	United Kingdom	20
Spain	United Kingdom	32	Germany	28
France	United Kingdom	17	Germany	15
Ireland	United Kingdom	61	United States	14
Italy	Germany	42	United Kingdom	8
Netherlands	Germany	49	United Kingdom	11
Portugal	United Kingdom	31	Germany	16

Source: EIBTM.

accessibility comes into its own. If the airlinks are in position on a scheduled basis, then destination choice is tied to frequency of flights and socially acceptable timetables. With the Caribbean, for example, UK groups normally choose Barbados on British Airways. The French opt for St Lucia on Air France. The Dutch go on KLM to the Dutch Antilles. The air schedules for each domestic carrier are well established in these former colonies. In 1994 the top outgoing incentive destination from Italy was the United States, but it had nothing to do with air access: Italy was competing in the 1994 soccer World Cup. It is not uncommon for Olympic Games destinations to show a huge upsurge in group travel interest in the few years following the Games, especially as new hotel facilities and tourist attractions may have been built to attract the Games in the first place. Barcelona, Sydney and Athens are illustrations of this.

INDIVIDUAL INCENTIVE TRAVEL

One significant trend is the growth of individual travel as an incentive. Strictly speaking this is not incentive travel, in terms of what the product characteristics should be. But in the United

States over one-third of all reward travel is individual, with over 60 per cent of US companies claiming to use it as a motivational device. This trend can be linked to the growth of flex plans (see Chapter 6), where performance-related points can be spent on family holidays rather than items like pensions or meal vouchers. Neither flex plans nor individual reward travel have yet made significant inroads into the European market, but it may only be a matter of time.

From research in the United States, we know that over 50 per cent of American qualifiers for incentive travel are repeat qualifiers. Everyday experience in Europe would seem to bear this out as a characteristic feature. The implication is that to achieve similar levels of performance improvement, creativity and analysis in the choice of destination is of paramount importance. Creativity includes the trend towards involvement of the qualifiers in some unique activity as part of the event, rather than simply organizing a passive tour. This is particularly true of European qualifiers, who tend to travel abroad much more than their US counterparts. They may be visiting a destination for the second or third time, and so will need a more creative activity or special venue than is normally provided to even the wealthy tourist.

Since the late 1980s there had been a reciprocation between the United States and Europe in terms of preferred incentive destination. The combination of the 1990 Gulf War and lower air fares across the Atlantic resulted in an unprecedented enthusiasm for US destinations from European buyers. However the aftermath of 9/11 and the introduction of increased security measures for visitors to the United States has caused a drop-off in numbers from Europe and the world in general. It has been easier to go closer to home than risk flying across the Atlantic when organizing an incentive travel event.

SIGNIFICANT PRODUCT FACTORS

Although this chapter sets out what characterizes successful incentive travel and some market statistics, it is worth taking note of what the qualifiers say. If they are not motivated to requalify, the product needs to be examined. Apart from the choice of destination, the significant elements of the incentive travel experience can be listed as follows:

- facility to bring their partner/spouse;
- recognition of achievement;
- free time in itinerary;
- hotel facilities;
- travel time.

These often-cited features of successful incentive travel will be true to varying degrees depending on the qualifier profile. It is important to recognize that the hotel facilities are of more concern to qualifiers than the destination itself. In research conducted at the University of Surrey, 'hotel facilities' came top of the list of major factors from UK-based incentive travel buyers, scoring twice as important as cultural backdrop or even the presence of a beach.

As people become more individual in their leisure tastes and more insular (take-away meals, home videos, personal stereos), group travel may well decline as a percentage of expenditure on rewards. There is certainly dramatic evidence in the United States that individual or family-oriented holiday rewards are growing fast and now account for as much as 30 per cent of all travel incentives, suggesting a mature product. Within Europe group incentive travel is still in its mid-growth phase, although market evidence from France and Italy reveals that individual incentive travel is becoming a significant part of any incentive or performance improvement proposal.

In global terms in excess of 15 per cent of the world's gross national product is involved with travel. In many countries travel and tourism is the biggest single employer. Growth in incentive travel, for both individuals and groups, is widely reported to be between 5 and 15 per cent, year on year, largely linked to a more travel and leisure-hungry economically developing world.

However, integrated performance improvement agencies would not recognize themselves as being part of the travel industry. Incentive travel will never account for more than 25 per cent of their total turnover, as we have already acknowledged that incentive travel is a marketing technique. Fulfilling the travel elements is incidental to the main task of motivating campaign participants to higher levels of job competence and performance improvement.

OTHER MEANS OF TRANSPORT

Trains

In considering incentive travel as a product, a brief word about trains is useful. Trains, which you can either charter or purchase individual tickets for, have limited use as a means of getting from one location to another. However, they can enhance a ground programme considerably, offering panoramas of a landscape often not possible by road. The journey from Montreux to Gstaad in Switzerland is not particularly remarkable by road, but by train the climb up into the high valleys offers unparalleled views of Lake Geneva, made even more memorable if you can use the train's restored Belle Epoque carriages.

The international success of the now restored Venice–Simplon Orient Express has given rise to many copycat products which sell well within their own incentives market (examples are the Palace on Wheels in India, the Blue Train, South Africa, the Royal Hungarian Express, Hungary and the Andalusian Express in Spain). But a note of caution should be sounded. Trains in all countries are run by strict timekeepers and custodians of protocol. You have to fit into their criteria, not the other way round. This can mean long waiting periods in sidings for no apparent reason, sequestering of specific trains for government use, and possibly questionable catering and service. You should check rigorously any get-out clauses in the event that your charter contract does not meet your expectations.

... and boats

Chartering boats is not new in incentive travel. It has become a standard element in any coastal or island-based programme. But using large commercial cruise ships for group incentives is relatively new. This is in line with the significant growth trend of consumer take-up of cruising, particularly with younger people. The advantage to the professional incentive organizer is tight control of the budget. Most cruise packages include virtually unlimited food and a generous drink allowance, complimentary on-board entertainment, with evening cabaret and a captive audience. As most cruise itineraries involve sailing at night and anchoring offshore or in port during the day, the ship becomes a floating hotel, with a different destination each day.

But as with all things nautical, some people react badly to being at sea, however gentle the motion (almost imperceptible with the largest vessels). Others may feel 'hemmed in' by being in such close proximity to other people. But in reality most research comparing expectations and experience of cruising shows that guests often comment how few people they thought were on board and how much more they enjoyed the experience than they expected.

You may also need to consider flight access and sailing times. If there are outbound flight delays, the ship will not wait for your group. Equally if the ship docks late at its final port of call, you could find you have lost your scheduled air seats home.

UK statistics reveal a healthy growth curve for cruising, which suggests that incentive participants would react well to the cruising concept. There are several ships available for private charter that are ideally suited to the incentive market (having a capacity of between 50 and 1,000 passengers), so the likelihood is that whole or part-ship charters for incentive events will become more common in the future, as the market develops and buyers become more comfortable with the concept of cruising.

FORWARD PLANNING OF DESTINATIONS

There is a temptation when planning your first incentive travel event to go for the most prestigious venue available. It is natural to want to achieve the biggest impact. However, incentive travel is often a medium to long-term technique which, if executed well, you will want to repeat. You need to consider carefully an outline plan for subsequent years.

For example, within Europe, Monte Carlo in one year would be difficult to follow up in year two to an unsophisticated audience. A more gradual progression over four years may be more appropriate as aspirations and expectations rise.

INCENTIVE TRAVEL PROGRESSION

Year 1	Year 2	Year 3	Year 4
Paris	Vienna	Rome	Monte Carlo

Inevitably you may consider medium or long-haul destinations once the nearer destinations have been used. Some experienced buyers into their tenth or more incentive travel event deliberately adopt a short-haul/long-haul rotation year on year, known to the participants, which allows them to 'come back' from long-haul to short-haul without fear of demotivation. Other users run long-haul destinations for the very top echelon, with short-haul destinations for the lower level of qualifiers. Another technique is to arrange extensions of three or four days at the same venue for the very highest achievers. Or they could fly on to another destination when the main group has returned home.

Whichever combination is used, each has its advantages and disadvantages, and these can be discussed with the incentives consultancy at the planning stage. The key point is not to go too far too soon, and to choose somewhere the participants will feel comfortable. A five-star hotel is no good if the main attraction of the event is social gatherings in the bar. The price of the round of drinks will become a hot topic of conversation which the organizer and the sponsor could do without.

SUMMARY

- Incentive travel is by far the most popular incentive reward after cash.
- Destination selection is an art as well as a science. Perception is everything.
- Ensure there is a planned promotional programme to enhance the destination appeal.
- The incentive travel product is not simply a more expensive consumer holiday product.
- Consider how you can create memories to encourage requalification the following year.
- Make a long-term plan for choice of destination if you intend to be a regular user of incentive travel.

1 Cottrell, N B (1972) 'Social facilitation' in *Experimental Social Psychology*, ed C G McClintock, Holt, Rinehart & Winston, New York.

8 | Tangibles: merchandise

With all my worldly goods I thee endow.

The marriage service

It is a significant fact that, although travel is highly perceived by participants as the most preferred reward choice after cash, much more money is spent on tangible items such as merchandise, vouchers and services. Most people start with merchandise when they construct their first incentive programme. The reason is not hard to find. Incentive travel is a big-ticket item per head (double if you include a partner), and is mainly used in industries where the volume of sales and product margins are high. Not every type of company can afford hosted travel events. In surveys, only 25 to 30 per cent of total performance improvement agency turnover was deemed to be incentive travel, leaving a significant amount being spent on other non-travel reward media. By a process of elimination this means merchandise, retail vouchers, services and domestic events.

MERCHANDISE CATALOGUES

Background

E F Macdonald (US), which was eventually bought by Carlson, was reputedly the first full-service motivation agency, offering a range of merchandise from printed catalogues in return for participant sales achievements. The pioneering campaigns were conducted in the United States as early as the 1930s, initially for the automotive industry in Detroit and then more widely for other business sectors. In the boom years after the Second World War, rising living standards and the growth of conspicuous consumption meant that offering specific merchandise items for sales achievements rather than more money made perfect sense. Being the first to acquire the latest home appliance was the upwardly mobile thing to do. Later, companies like Maritz and BI (Business Incentives) exploited the newly affluent corporate sector in the United States, and today they employ thousands of staff to manage performance improvement programmes around the world.

The very latest electronic gadgets, labour-saving devices or designer goods can be packaged together as a merchandise catalogue, sold for a nominal sum to the client to distribute to participants, with a simple leaflet explaining how many 'points' are required for each item. The more you sell, the more reward you earn.

In the heyday of catalogue programmes, motivation houses and incentive agencies would buy stock at wholesale prices, storing the goods at distribution centres to dispatch to campaign claimants. By selling the goods on to clients at retail prices less a small discount they could make significant profit margins. However, in the late 1980s such holding of stock became gradually less viable. Participants had become much more discerning considering the price and value of catalogue goods, comparing items with what was readily available from their local stores. The wider distribution of consumer goods, particularly from out-of-town sites and superstores, has meant that speed of delivery has become a key factor, as incentive organizers try to close the gap between the desired behaviour pattern and the reward. In theory, the quicker, the better.

As an alternative to holding stock, with all the inherent risks of being stuck with unpopular or obsolete items, some motivation houses set up rolling accounts with the big mail-order catalogue companies to supply goods on a JIT (just in time) basis, through specific 'incentive teams' within the mail-order companies. However, the drop in demand during the early 1990s caused mail-order companies to reduce the range of items available, and in some cases cease the service altogether. For many suppliers of merchandise the internet has changed the business model from being a printed catalogue provider to allowing customers to order online.

The rise of retail vouchers with their quasi-cash advantages – any denomination, easy distribution, wide range of redemption possibilities – triggered a reappraisal of 'the catalogue' as a product to deliver reward. It is well known that, given an equal choice between merchandise from a catalogue and vouchers, over 75 per cent of participants invariably choose retail vouchers nowadays.

Advantages and disadvantages

But before we condemn all merchandise schemes out of hand it is worth outlining the advantages and disadvantages of merchandise catalogue schemes in general. (See Table 8.1.)

Table 8.1 Advantages and disadvantages of merchandise schemes

Advantages	Disadvantages
Show each item on offer	Often a limited range
Colour presentation	Cost of colour catalogue
Distribution of catalogue by mail	Impersonal
Items priced in 'points'	Difficult to assess real value
No need to visit shop	Delays in delivery
Minimal client administration	Lack of client 'ownership'
Transit repair guarantees	Inconvenient to return goods
Lower costs	Many goods unbranded

From an incentive organizer's viewpoint, catalogues are simple to purchase and distribute, but there are some significant disadvantages for participants. The most obvious factor is the delay in distribution of the goods. It normally takes two to three weeks after the qualifying period to confirm sales made. In most programmes, a communication is then dispatched to the participant, saying how many points have been won. The participant chooses an award by completing a claim form, which is mailed to the distribution/fulfilment house. This process is increasingly being facilitated through dedicated websites, where participants can order online and view their selections without the need for a catalogue. Unless stock is being held by the fulfilment house (less and less common) an order will then be dispatched to the item stockist. As such items tend to be 'picked' on a cycle basis, the order may have to wait for the next picking cycle. In some cases, the item requested may not be in stock. The item then needs to be delivered by road under contract to the claimant. No wonder most catalogue schemes carry the proviso of 28 days for delivery.

In commercial terms it has to be said that for the merchandise supplier incentive-related merchandise is a very small market compared with the entire consumer mail-order market. This is reflected in the less than perfect delivery concessions made by the supplying companies. It all boils down to what represents core business for the supplier. Unless the product supplier specializes in 'incentive reward products', there will always be tension between supplying mass-market products on a regular basis to consumers and supplying incentive rewards to individual home addresses on an irregular basis.

Another problem often perceived by participants is the limited range of goods being offered. This stems from the fact that the incentive organizer is often working six to nine months in advance of the redemption process. Many campaign participants tend to accumulate their reward points during the campaign and spend them at the end of the campaign. To ensure that participants can actually receive the items they have worked so hard for, the supplier needs to guarantee that the items in the catalogue will be available in sufficient quantities. As most mail-order companies contract for stock twice a year for consumers, in most cases incentive participants are not able to obtain automatically the items in the launch catalogue. The solution? A limited range of goods is offered by the mail-order companies or other suppliers, comprising items they can guarantee to have in stock. The result? A rather bland selection of middle-of-the-road items which neither inspire nor excite higher-level participants.

Catalogue production costs

Colour brochures are expensive to produce and the more images there are per page, the more expensive the brochure. Catalogues provide the worst possible scenario if you want to keep incentive promotional costs down. Lots of separate pictures means lots of detailed copy and short print runs. (Most client campaigns require less than 1,000 copies of the promotional material.)

One way to circumvent this problem has been to use the supplier's catalogue which has been produced in bulk specifically for the incentives market. To personalize it, you simply overprint the cover or supply a completely new cover, to include your incentive campaign logo and details of how participants can qualify. This is fine if you are running a campaign for your own sales force or administration team. However, if you are one of many suppliers attempting to gain additional market share from a distributor (car dealer, retailer) who sells other people's goods too, you could find your 'catalogue' is the same as a rival's catalogue, bar the outer cover, thereby negating any competitive advantage in running the incentive scheme.

Bespoke catalogues are a better answer, but you need to have a participant universe of at lease 5,000 to make one viable. The production cost of the catalogue could be more than the reward budget, and certainly more than any incremental profit from the incentive programme.

Where there's a will ...

There are ingenious ways to get around the inherent problems with merchandise catalogues, all of which are valid. (See Table 8.2.)

Table 8.2 Problems and solutions

Problem	Solution
Limited range	Promote a few key items and simply list other related products as text
Cost of catalogues	Build the cost into the participant reward points
Delivery delays	Set up a hotline for telephone claimants
Lack of client branding	Personalize the cover
Unbranded goods	Emphasize value for money
Goods too expensive for the campaign rules	Earmark expensive items as 'star prizes' awarded mid-campaign

Most of the disadvantages of catalogues are to do with presentation. Each audience needs to be considered separately and the appropriate merchandise catalogue chosen. Perhaps the most important characteristic of catalogues is that they are a very blunt incentive mechanism designed to appeal to a wide cross-section. They usually contain a varied range of items to attract the widest possible band of participants. But in doing so they can become untargeted and impersonal.

When to use printed catalogues

Catalogues do have their uses, but they are more shotgun than rifle if they are being used as an incentive reward mechanism.

Small universe of participants

Provided the catalogue has been produced by the incentive supplier in large quantities, you can usually buy a good-quality colour catalogue at a low unit price, even if you have just a small number of participants. If you are setting up an incentive scheme for fewer than 100 potential participants, a catalogue with an accompanying letter detailing the reward points mechanism is certainly a rapid and cost-effective way to get colour promotional materials into the hands of participants with the minimum of administrative investment.

Diverse universe of participants

If your target audience is diverse in terms of geographic spread, range of income or volume of sales, a catalogue can provide a catch-all solution as to what to offer as an incentive. Participants can choose items to suit themselves, within the range offered.

Loyalty building

If your aim is to establish medium to long-term loyalty in the purchase of your product or with franchised employees, a catalogue can help participants accumulate points over a relatively long period. By involving participants' partners in the choice of item (by mailing to the home address and writing to both partners), you can extend the life of the campaign considerably and forge a strong bond between sponsor and participant.

Burger King Corporation

All 41,000 Burger King associates qualify for long-service awards in the form of a selection of branded and customized merchandise appropriate to the number of years of service. Participants build up credits over the years which can be redeemed for jewellery, sporting goods, household accessories, electronic goods and, in later years, holidays around the world. A toll-free (free-phone) number is used for communication and merchandise selection.

Middle-band participants

If you know your top providers and have already decided to run an incentive travel event for them, a catalogue could be a good compromise for the middle-band category, who will at least be able to earn some reward, however small. Perception that you can win something, however small, from the campaign is always important.

In broad terms catalogues are really for participants you do not know very well, but still need to incentivize in a volume-related sales campaign. Catalogues are a broad-brush reward solution in the absence of a detailed profile of the universe. In terms of effectiveness, they tend to work best in conjunction with other rewards or techniques (additional travel event, double points for the first month, quarterly bonus prizes, lottery element), because as stand-alone incentives they can appear somewhat dated and unfocused to audiences who are well used to incentive programmes.

INVENT YOUR OWN CATALOGUE!

If you are not happy with the choice of items in an off-the-shelf catalogue or are worried that the spread of values does not reflect the earning capacity of points in your particular scheme (no point in having hi-fi systems on offer if the highest reward points achievable are worth £50), you could choose your own selection of merchandise. This technique is often used for consumers such as petrol forecourt promotions where five or more levels of award are chosen. The participants choose an award depending on their spend, but the items on offer are hardly motivational and relatively disposable. If you do choose your own selection of merchandise to suit your audience, you will face the same dilemmas as the big mail-order companies.

QUESTIONS TO CONSIDER IF YOU CREATE YOUR OWN
CATALOGUE

- What is the profile of the audience?
- What items will complement their lifestyle?
- How much will they be able to redeem from the campaign?

- Will the items be available when they want to redeem?
- Will there be enough of each item available?
- Can I get a better price than buying the item retail?
- What is the cost of delivery?
- What is the policy on damaged or returned goods?
- What is the policy on substitute models, alternative colours?
- How do I deal with cross-border international winners?
- What is the policy if someone claims they never received the item?

Many of these problems are to do with the decision to hold stock or not. One way around buying items up front in the hope that the participants will choose as you expect is to set up call-off arrangements from a range of suppliers as and when participants claim. However, there is always the risk that the item is no longer available at the price you set in your budget. The administration of setting up deals with 10 or more separate award suppliers is not very efficient. What was originally going to be a 'simple' incentive offering a few dozen specific rewards suitable for your participants can easily turn into an administrative nightmare with the potential to cause more harm than good.

Catalogues are good catch-all reward media for a diverse audience which requires minimum administration. They provide the opportunity to promote the campaign with stylish colour material, even to a small group of participants at low cost per head. However, because they need to appeal to a wide audience, the items offered tend to be bland, lacking in aspirational value and not of top-brand quality. It has to be said that catalogues can be perceived, among regular incentive users, as being old-fashioned and somewhat out of date as an effective reward medium, particularly with the development of web-based reward-delivery systems (see Chapter 9).

SUMMARY

- Catalogues provide an inexpensive way to market desirable goods.
- But the time-lag between claiming and receiving can be negative.
- If used for the right audience or as a first-time incentive, they can be effective.
- But they are a relatively blunt motivational tool with an 'old-fashioned' image.
- In time they may well become obsolete, as web-based schemes become more widely available.

9

Tangibles: vouchers and services

Fair exchange is no robbery.

Proverb

You can now use retail vouchers in exchange for almost every conceivable product or service from childcare to funeral costs. But why are vouchers so popular in incentive campaigns compared with cash or merchandise? They are cheaper. They are virtually instant. The are multi-denominational. In other words they have all the flexibility of cash with none of the messiness associated with delivering merchandise. When 75 per cent or more of campaign participants choose vouchers whenever they get an equal choice between vouchers and merchandise, the perceived benefits must be considerable. Voucher sales in the United Kingdom exceeded £1.35 billion in the first quarter of 2004, representing an 8.9 per cent increase over the previous year, dwarfing by some margin the marketing budgets spent on merchandise or incentive travel.

We covered the case against cash in Chapter 5. It is now worth stating the case for vouchers so that we can consider merchandise options in their true light.

ADVANTAGES OF VOUCHERS

Speed of issue

One of the basic tenets of motivation is to provide reward as closely as possible in time to the desired behaviour so as to reinforce that behaviour in the future. Provided you have written adequate claim procedures, vouchers can be as quick to issue as cash, often quicker as distribution does not necessarily depend on payroll routines. Vouchers are certainly easier to distribute than merchandise and have none of the associated mechanical problems of transit damage, the participant not being at home at delivery time or simply not liking the item when it (finally) arrives.

Vouchers can be sent direct to the participant following a telephone claim. In some circumstances there may be sound motivational value in sending the vouchers to the local manager or line supervisor so that they can be presented in front of the participant's peers as a positive recognition opportunity.

Vouchers can be bought in advance and retained locally to use as soon as the desired improvement takes place. Many non-sales staff have benefited from voucher awards for achieving standards of attendance (combating absenteeism), hitting team productivity goals, improving customer service standards or rewarding efficiency suggestions. Even sales people can be encouraged to take administration seriously, using vouchers as the incentive.

A major loan company was concerned at the low levels of acceptance at head office of the new legally required Customer Needs Analysis (CNA) forms completed by its sales people. If completion rates did not improve, the regulators of the industry could impose heavy fines or even take the sales people out of the field for specific retraining. A three-month incentive programme was devised, using additional training and incentives to focus attention on this deficiency in the sales process. Participants competed to gain one of 10 top places in a series of regional leagues, with a specific amount of vouchers as the reward. There was a wide range of participant geographic locations and earnings. The campaign was simple but effective. 'Right First Time' improved CNA acceptance from 55 to 74 per cent, with some branches achieving 87 per cent, with a minimum of administrative costs.

Multi-denominational

Like cash, vouchers come in all denominations so they are flexible down to the smallest increment if you need to reward performance improvement exactly. Participants can add their own cash to the award if they wish to purchase items priced higher than their award. They can also receive change if there is a small discrepancy in the retail goods price.

You do not need to hold voucher stock unless you want to. Dispatch to participants can be by mail or through the line manager. Vouchers are easy to take home on the day the participant wins the award. They can even be spent on the same day, if required.

Flexibility is the key

But above all, vouchers provide the reward medium which matches ideally the personal aspirations of the participants. Because the participant chooses how to redeem the vouchers, you do not need to consider whether the catalogue reflects the profile of the participants, or what items to buy in and promote for a specific campaign.

As we move towards a cashless society it is remarkable how many products and services can now be purchased using vouchers. Here are just a few examples:

- holidays;
- food;
- childcare;
- gardening equipment;
- books;
- DIY items;

- health club membership;
- utility (such as gas) expenses;
- clothes;
- alcohol;
- hotel rooms;
- department store items;
- restaurant meals;
- sports equipment;
- music;
- television licence;
- petrol.

It is now possible to pay for around 75 per cent of all regular expenditure using voucher systems. With vouchers sold at face value or less if purchased in bulk, they represent a most efficient way to deliver the reward. However, redemption is an important factor for participants.

REDEEMING FEATURES: 'UNIVERSAL' VOUCHERS

All voucher systems rely on prompt redemption in the same way that the economy relies on money in the banking system. Vouchers are no good if retail assistants are not trained to redeem them. There is usually no problem with specific retail vouchers. If the logo on the shop front matches the logo on the vouchers, there is a high probability that you will be able to use them like cash.

However 'universal vouchers' are a different matter altogether. Not only do they cost more (upwards of 5 per cent of face value depending on the volume purchased), there is always the potential problem that some retail assistants will not have been trained to accept the vouchers, causing embarrassment to both the award winner and retail staff. Universal voucher companies rely on the USP (unique selling point) of one voucher which can be redeemed in a variety of unrelated outlets. But like credit card acceptance, allegiances can change overnight.

One further problem is the spread of outlets covered. Some universal voucher providers claim acceptance in 'over 10,000 outlets', which should be enough for most participants' needs. However, in practice you may find that the geographic distribution of retailers in the scheme is skewed to the north or the south, or wherever, depending on the assiduousness of the voucher field sales force during the previous year. This can lead to a significant number of winners not being able to redeem their universal vouchers without a lengthy car journey.

Popular vouchers

Each participant base tends to exhibit specific redeeming characteristics, given an open choice of retail vouchers, although there are some common features. In the United Kingdom, Marks & Spencer (high-quality clothes/food retailer) and Thomas Cook (holidays) are always highly placed, and represent together at least 20 per cent of the total retail voucher market. This supports the view that if positioned properly, participants will use vouchers to reward themselves in aspirational ways rather than simply fund everyday expenses. You can encourage this by offering only vouchers that can be redeemed for high-quality goods or aspirational items.

But this is not always the case. Voucher choice often reflects the state of the economy, so in recessionary times vouchers are often used as cash substitutes. This is evident in the growth of utility vouchers, food retailer vouchers and petrol vouchers. However, as the economy recovers, such options tend to be less popular.

DISADVANTAGES OF VOUCHERS

One possible disadvantage of using vouchers is cash flow. Because vouchers are the equivalent of cash as far as retailers are concerned, they need to be purchased upfront. No one can predict the success of an incentive programme or the choices the winners will make at the outset of a campaign. This leads to buying voucher stock at irregular intervals during the programme to fulfil requests. You could be left holding non-returnable stock if you buy too much of one type too early. This problem can be solved by buying through an incentive house, which habitually stocks all the leading vouchers and keeps a rolling selection available for a handling fee.

ADMINISTRATION

Voucher administration needs careful planning if you have a large universe of participants. The combination of a wide range of retail vouchers and making them available in small denominations results in a highly complex tracking procedure, which needs to be as tight as any payroll system. The key features of such a system are:

- Each participant needs a unique number code.
- Each voucher needs a unique number code.
- Each allocation needs to be dated.
- Each distribution needs to be recorded.

From the sponsor's point of view, you need to be able to track which voucher was sent to which participant on any designated date. This enables you to prove vouchers were actually dispatched and received (if you use a recorded delivery service) if a query arises. The participant needs to be able to identify whether a voucher request has been actioned and if so, where and when it was dispatched.

With most voucher suppliers, discounts are based on achieving bulk purchase thresholds. By tracking voucher redemptions on a daily basis, you may be able to qualify for higher overall discounts by buying stock forward to push you into the higher discount bracket, even if you have no immediate redemptions for that additional stock.

At some stage you may have to account for tax on vouchers issued to each recipient. By tracking dispatches on an individual basis the information will be readily available so that tax paid certificates can be issued to participants promptly and accurately.

VOUCHER PROMOTION

One of the few advantages of merchandise catalogues is colour pictures of the goods on offer. Vouchers by themselves are little more than alternative paper money. There is always the danger that voucher incentives will fall flat because there is too much emphasis on the feature (easy exchange medium) and not enough on the benefit (what they buy). In the final analysis a voucher is only a means to an end. It enables you to obtain the reward you want as quickly as possible. In itself, a voucher is a pretty dull piece of paper or in some cases merely an electronic credit.

So when you come to promote vouchers as part of an incentive campaign:

- Concentrate on what the vouchers can be exchanged for.
- Emphasize the wide choice.
- Emphasize the speed of redemption, (immediate).
- Emphasize the convenience of local redemption.
- Emphasize their collectability – the 'save up for something big' feature.

It is noticeable that universal vouchers tend to feature strongly the range of retail outlets they cover, rather than what they can be redeemed for. Some companies offer a personalization service to overprint an existing retail outlets brochure. This is nonsense. Participants only need to know where they can redeem their vouchers (or bonds as they call them) as mechanical information. The important benefit is what they can buy, so emphasize the reward not the delivery system.

'DESIGNER AWARDS'

On both sides of the Atlantic, there are many examples of delivering reward in unusual ways. One approach is to follow the logic of offering as wide a choice as possible by simply allowing participants to accumulate points and for them to choose exactly what they want. Participants then ring a telephone hotline to obtain a quote on an item or service of their choice. It could be a specific holiday, having the house decorated, tickets for an opera, getting the car valeted or a meal for two at a top restaurant. The ideas are unlimited. The essential point is that participants design their own reward and work towards a personal goal.

'Designer awards', as they are known, are increasing in popularity as people become more individual in their needs and circumstances. Not everyone lives in a nuclear family environment. In promotional terms, spelling out the unlimited choice concept needs to be done clearly, showing examples of what designer awards are possible with perhaps ballpark prices. Experience shows that even by offering unlimited choice, you still find most of the participants choosing the voucher route. But the unusual ideas generated by the remaining minority provide superb promotional stories to market to the participant database to prompt more imaginative redemption.

DEVELOPING TECHNOLOGY

The image of a consumer catalogue and the range of goods (rather than goods and services) may not suit all participants to the same degree. Vouchers are now the preferred way to redeem incentive campaign rewards for most participants because they are as flexible as cash, and can be redeemed quickly and locally. The plethora of retail and service vouchers now available means that virtually anything in a merchandise catalogue can be obtained through a voucher system.

However the key to a successful incentive campaign is timely and clear communication. Developments using the internet have changed the way employee benefits are administrated in recent years, and much the same is happening in the area of rewards administration, whether the fulfilment is merchandise, vouchers or services. The best way to explain the new trend is by an example.

I am grateful to P&MM for access to details about its Rewardbanking product, which is a good illustration of how to manage the intranet/internet model of keeping participants informed and delivering the reward on an individual participant basis.

Intranet/internet communication

The bad old days of preparing printed bulletins with masses of figures on a monthly basis are long gone for experienced users of motivational programmes. With the advent of the internet has come the opportunity to launch, explain and communicate with participants on a real-time basis for the first time. P&MM's Rewardbanking product is just one example of several products now available in the market.

A standard suite of web pages has been produced which can be quickly personalized for any corporate sponsor. Qualifying participants gain access to the site using a password and in some cases by verifying their personal details too. Once they are logged on, participants have access to over 800 reward items ranging from merchandise and holidays through to vouchers and services. They even have a 'dream' option, a type of designer award, by which qualifiers can nominate what they want to spend their reward points on. A typical home page would include seasonal reward offers and a 'news' section which can either be campaign-specific or sponsor-specific, such as new product details or information in the press.

Functionality is a key feature of the system. Participants need to be able to see what is on offer, compare items, check their points and be able to redeem online on a 24/7 basis. They also need to be able to ask questions and change their minds from time to time. To assist the sponsor, there is a full suite of management reports, including the number of hits the site receives, analysis of who has ordered what, points achieved by participants and full tax and national insurance reporting for payroll purposes.

Once the participant is on the site, one click throws up the choices of product on offer and the points value. (See Figures 9.1

Figure 9.1 Rewardbanking options

Figure 9.2 Rewardbanking kitchenware products

and 9.2.) If the participant decides on a particular item it can be 'added to basket' in the same way that most ordering is done on the internet, and browsing can continue. A useful advantage over printed catalogues is the facility to offer event-based products,

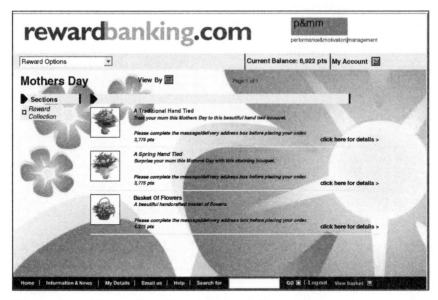

Figure 9.3   Rewardbanking Mother's Day offers

such as Christmas gifts or items suitable for Mother's Day (see Figure 9.3.)

Because the communication channel is virtually instant you have the facility as the sponsor to send corporate messages, announce leaders, change the points levels and issue general gee-up messages whenever they are needed. (See Figure 9.4.) The same channel can also be used to do instant research on what participants feel about the rewards and even the incentive scheme in general, rather than having to conduct more formal research at the end of the programme.

Security is clearly a key issue. The system encrypts all personal data as it is sent over the web to the same standard as the technology used for credit card information. Personal data is then stored on a separate server complete with firewall protection. There is a disaster recovery system to ensure that the site can continue to function in the event of unforeseen circumstances.

Costs vary according to the supplier you choose, but most levy a set-up charge and then a fee per participant. The participants' fee is a function of how many you want to include in the programme,

Figure 9.4 Rewardbanking information and news

and there may be minimum charges for smaller-participant databases. There may also be a charge for management reports depending on how complex they are. There will be a contingency fee for the rewards being redeemed and extra charges for updating campaign news or for providing a hotline answered with the sponsor's name. The good news for financial directors is that the facility costs are likely to be much less than for creating a bespoke printed catalogue.

There is no doubt that the marketing and human resources communities are opting for web-based facilities as standard when it comes to reward redemption. The P&MM system includes the option for participants to take advantage of voice recognition technology (IVR: interactive voice response) whereby they can ask for their balance of reward points and the amount is read back to them over the phone. They can then go on to order vouchers using the phone keypad. With further developments in mobile phone technology it will not be long before full access to reward sites and remote ordering will be possible 'on the move' for busy participants. In addition the introduction of 'chip and PIN' credit cards in

Europe will improve the ability to redeem some goods and services through retail stores in a number of countries, perhaps without even having to visit the reward site itself.

In the United States plastic gift cards have replaced 90 per cent of all paper voucher schemes, and provided retailers can be persuaded to accept them, the future of vouchers is more likely to be electronic rather than paper, although at the moment plastic cards are still proving to be more expensive to produce and issue. Several communication suites now offer the option to run the same reward programme cross-border, with or without translation, depending on the availability of local reward suppliers. So doing campaigns across several country groups is now relatively straightforward, with all the computerized administration being done back in the sponsoring or host country.

SUMMARY

- Vouchers are less expensive than cash to provide.
- Vouchers provide instant gratification and can be used for almost all regular purchases.
- Beware of some 'universal' vouchers in terms of their redeemability.
- Promote what vouchers can buy, not the voucher itself.
- 'Designer awards' offer the ultimate in choice for individuals.
- Online reward systems are fast becoming the standard way to promote and redeem rewards.
- In the future redemption may well be through wireless technology and smart cards if retailers can be persuaded to participate.

10

Events

There's no such thing as a free lunch.

Milton Friedman

Merchandise and vouchers are in general individual awards which participants redeem for personal effort. However, reward does not always need to be something you enjoy alone or just with close family. Hosted events can be a powerful motivational tool in promoting performance improvement. If the event is overseas, it becomes incentive travel (see Chapter 7). At home, the same disciplines apply, but because they tend to be smaller affairs, the emphasis is much more on recognition than logistics.

But why run an event? What is its motivational appeal? Where do events fit in the panoply of incentive rewards or indeed general corporate communication? There are several kinds of motivational event:

- sales conferences;
- hosted weekend incentives;
- individual, unhosted breaks;
- group activities;
- staff parties.

MEETINGS AND CONFERENCES

Even though individuals may not have to qualify in performance terms to attend a domestic conference (although many do have to), it can play a valuable part in the motivation and performance improvement strategy of a business. Yet all too often regular conferences only pay lip service to communication, fulfilling only one side of the bargain – the directors directing the directed.

Communication is by definition a two-way process. Even in the most cost-conscious companies, it is recognized that the financial investment represented by the aggregate loss of productive human hours away from the field and the costs of staging the event is money well spent. As a motivational tool a conference serves many purposes:

- to pass on strategic direction;
- to create a channel for feedback;
- to launch new initiatives;
- to recognize top achievers;
- to establish new working practices;
- to promote teamwork;
- to stem harmful rumours (they can deal with negative issues too).

The first thing to establish is what purpose the conference serves. It may act as a focal point for annual planning and budgeting, to ensure all essential plans are completed in time. It may be vital as the only opportunity in a year to report from board level to junior employees on the progress of the company. It could be used purely as a gee-up device for the sales force, to recognize high achievers and spur them on to better things. It could be the culmination of a series of smaller managerial meetings where the decisions made are then cascaded down to the rest of the organization. But whatever the main reason, there should actually be a reason, not just habit or that time of year again.

If performance improvement = knowledge × incentive × communication, then the conference is not optional. It is essential for sound motivation.

Table 10.1 Percentage of conference bednights booked in an average year

Month	%	Rank order
July	7.3	1 November
August	3.4	2 October
September	9.8	3 September
October	10.7	4 April
November	10.8	5 March
December	8.3	6 June
January	7.6	7 December
February	7.6	8 January
March	8.9	9 February
April	9.6	10 May
May	7.4	11 July
June	8.6	12 August

Cost efficiency

Although most conferences are impossible to quantify in incremental revenue terms, there is no doubt that many conferences are designed to produce a specific business result. Intentia International ran a worldwide roadshow which visited 33 venues across four continents, presenting new products to audiences of from 40 to 1,500 participants. Flexible, portable staging was designed to cope with the varying dimensions of the chosen venues. A virtual presenter, Mr James Ponda, a computer-generated frog, became a global hit with audiences around the world. Twelve systems were sold as a direct result of the presentations, providing gross revenues of £50 million. The cost of the entire roadshow was less than £500,000.

Timing

So when should you have a conference? Table 10.1 shows the number of conference bednights booked by a major hotel chain in a normal year. It is a good indication of conference booking habits in general.

From this analysis it is clear that most conferences are held in the autumn, with a second tranche taking place in the spring. There are very few conferences in August. This distribution suggests that the main rationale for holding the annual conference is to review the year and launch the next fiscal year's initiatives. (Company years are usually January to December or April to March.) However, apart from August, there's not much difference statistically on a month-by-month basis.

But it does not follow that every company should run its conference in the spring or autumn. You should hold your conference at the most suitable time of the year to support the main aim of the exercise. Toy retailers tend to run conferences in the spring or summer, as new stock for Christmas needs to be sold into retailers well before the autumn. Pharmaceutical companies and computer dealers work in a fast-moving product development environment. Quarterly meetings may be more appropriate than an annual address. Financial services tend to follow the traditional annual reporting cycle of April to March, suggesting a conference in April or May to be ideal.

Conference content

Once the date and the main objectives have been decided, the next thing to consider is the content. Great care must be taken to build a programme to appeal across several levels, not just at the level of those speaking. A board used to having its own way with very little dialogue down the line is likely to produce a conference akin to a party political television broadcast, with most viewers turning off. The converse is also true. If the job of organizing the conference is given to a relatively junior executive with little feel for the corporate culture, you are likely to end up with a very enjoyable event full of sound and fury but signifying very little when it comes to content. The content has to include a careful balance of messages to support the main objectives, and provide the opportunity to share ideas or at least show openness to a consultative approach.

A checklist may help the organizing committee focus their thoughts on what sort of conference they want.

CONFERENCE CHECKLIST

- The main purpose of the conference.
- How to measure its success.
- Audience profile.
- Proposed length of the presentations.
- Political/cultural environment of the business.
- Five main messages in order of importance.
- Pace of the presentations.
- Overall style (dramatic, businesslike, chat show and so on).
- Need to incorporate existing materials/logos.
- Any elements to be carried over to future presentations.
- Specific equipment requirements (videos, slides, prompting and so on).
- Planning schedule/deadlines.
- Authority for signing off ideas costs.
- Budget parameters.

By answering these questions, however informally, you will have gone a considerable way to condensing the brief for production specialists to consider. Motivational elements are important – it should not be purely information provision. This is particularly true of the choice of theme.

Theme

A conference theme is important for both content and style, as it helps to clarify the main messages and identify a dominant image for the audience to take away with them at the end of the day. Themes are very subjective. They work best if they are ambiguous and tie in with the current mood of the company culture or market. Here are just some examples of themes which have been used in a variety of industries.

- Embark on Excellence
- Going Places
- Question of Quality
- Against Adversity
- New Horizons
- Breaking the Barriers
- The Express to Success
- Facing the Future
- Theory into Practice
- Go for Gold
- Counting on Customers
- People before Profit
- Mission: Improvement
- No Compromise
- Who Dares Wins
- Ideas in Action
- Leading the Way
- Building on Strength
- Today, Tomorrow
- Charting the Future
- Committed to Quality
- Driving Force
- Quality Counts
- Future Perfect
- Winner Takes All
- Satisfaction Guaranteed
- People Matter Most
- Service First
- The Bottom Line
- Winning Through
- Quest for the Best
- On Course for Quality
- The Power to Deliver
- Steps to Success.

Most work best if they have some specific meaning for the company or its culture. In a sales conference environment where you may be launching a new travel incentive, some veiled reference to an exotic overseas destination in the conference theme can help to underline the highlight of the day in the memories of those who attended (such as The Road to Rio, or Going Places).

Structuring the conference

As with any presentation, whether verbal, printed or in conference, you need to develop a structure to emphasize the main messages in the most efficient way. There are several techniques you may want to consider.

- **Syndicate sessions.** In these delegates are broken up into smaller groups with a facilitator to discuss specific issues and brought back into the main conference to report on their deliberations.
- **Celebrity compere.** A professional link person or television celebrity introduces the various speakers and interviews the top executives, asking difficult questions the audience perhaps may not want to be seen to be asking.

- **Chat show format.** Speakers give their message in conversation with the compere rather than formally from a lectern.
- **Motivational speakers.** Famous sports personalities, explorers, achievers of all kinds tell the audience how they managed to achieve so highly, providing strong messages of preparation, teamwork and dedication to the goal.
- **Audience interaction.** Each member of the audience can press a button by his or her seat to respond to general questions from the stage, as in a game show.

The day needs to be planned to provide peaks of interest to keep the audience listening. You may decide to save your best internal speaker until the session before lunch to end the morning on a high note and provide talking points for delegates over lunch. The notorious graveyard session after lunch (where the audience sleep off their lunch) should be targeted as a participatory or high-interest session (such as the guest motivational speaker) to keep the audience engaged. If you do have specific information to present from technical departments, you should consider whether the detail could be a handout at the end of the day and the main technical message communicated as a video module in the style of news reportage, or try an interview session. Too many conferences are spoiled by technical supremos who cannot present.

A keynote speech from the leader is often billed as the last item. In most businesses this works well, providing an all-encompassing view from the top in terms that every individual can understand. However, it is not always desirable to have the top gun as the compere. In fact, it detracts from the keynote speech if a few hours earlier the compere has been talking about departure details or the arrangements for coffee. A professional link person is worth their weight in gold, and they do not necessarily need to be a national television personality to command attention.

Motivational matters

In motivational terms, any internal or distributor conference should confine itself to matters of direct relevance to the audience, discarding any tendency to include 'head office' items unless they are necessary to an understanding of the message. The principle of 'What's in it for me?' is as good a guide as any to what to include on the agenda. If the item does not help to improve motivation or stimulate higher performance, you should question why it is on the agenda in the first place.

It has been said more than once that a great idea for a sales conference is to hire an empty hall and simply let the delegates talk to each other for six hours. That way they get to learn 'best practice' without interference from the stage. Recognizing that sales delegates want as many useful ideas as you can cram in to the allotted time is important when you decide what content to include or reject.

Finally, there is always the opportunity to recognize top performers at a staff or sales conference, so some thought needs to go into what may be appropriate. It may be practical to show pictures or text of top performers on screen, get them to stand up and take a bow in their seats, or even arrange for some of them to be officially recognized on stage. The key point is to ensure that the figures are correct, the pictures are in the right sequence and they are being recognized for the right reasons. Including the name of the representative from a local office could all go sour, if he was dismissed yesterday for gross misconduct. The recognition on stage could be accompanied by the presentation of a plaque or certificate, but remember to have a photographer on hand so that the moment can be recycled the following month in the company newsletter.

HOSTED WEEKEND INCENTIVES

Weekend incentives at a top hotel or a historic house hosted by the company have become an integral part of many sales incentives to support a longer-term incentive travel programme. Typically the very top performers over 12 months qualify for an overseas travel incentive, but 12 months is a long time to keep the message fresh. Many companies add quarterly or four-month mini-campaigns during the 12-month cycle to focus effort on key cyclical activities (prospecting, specific seasonal products, quality processes) to keep interest alive. One reward strategy is to set up a small, hosted weekend which is a mirror image of the overseas travel event, to encourage the weekend qualifiers to strive for the end-of-year event. Clearly secondary rewards (vouchers or merchandise) can be built into the mini-campaign for those who do not qualify for the event itself.

Although they are generally small, attention to detail for weekend events is important, particularly if there are fewer than 20 guests. Conversation can be awkward for a group who do not know each other, so hosting the event is vital to its success. It helps to have a guest list, with perhaps a two or three-line 'biography' to encourage people to talk. The company hosts should take the lead through a welcome speech, full involvement in the programme, and a proprietorial approach to service and smooth organization. After all, the guests have risen to the top of their particular tree and they expect to be treated as winners.

Opinions differ about the type of programme to run. Should it be a go-as-you-please weekend, only meeting up with the other guests for dinner, or should every moment be packed with incident and activity? As usual, the answer is a compromise. A typical programme which works well might read as follows.

Friday	Check in, individually from 3.00 pm.
19.30 hrs	Cocktails in the bar, introductions.
20.15 hrs	Dinner in a private room, low-key cabaret or an entertaining speaker.
Saturday	Morning excursion or activity for everyone. Lunch en route. Afternoon free for recuperation, using the hotel leisure facilities, preparing for dinner.
19.30 hrs	Private cocktails.
20.15 hrs	Gala dinner in a different (more spectacular) room with memorable cabaret, music, dancing if appropriate.
Sunday	Breakfast at leisure. Depart individually before noon. (Or offer a light lunch, with final thank yous before departure.)

With this type of format, there is an opportunity to get to know the other guests early on, but there is also time to relax on an individual basis.

GROUP ACTIVITIES

Depending on the profile of the winners, participation days or weekends can be a good way to reward effort and promote teamwork, particularly for staff or singles (those without partners). There are many options available, limited only by the imagination of organizers and the willingness of the invitees to participate. Here are some examples.

- **Murder mystery.** Guests try to solve clues to a murder, by gathering evidence and talking to hired actors who stay in character during the entire event. This can be done as a dinner entertainment which begins at cocktails and ends at midnight, with a whodunit conference next day in the library after breakfast.
- **Indoor problem solving.** Teams are given information, some kind of objective and a currency resource to promote working together towards a common goal in competition with other teams. Usually dressed in some kind of theme ('You are all treasure-seekers …'), they provide an entertaining two or three hours with plenty of opportunity to practise analysis and teamwork skills.
- **Outdoor problem solving.** Teams tackle a range of physical problems to win points in a competitive environment. Typically this includes taking apparently unrelated equipment (rope, barrel, plank, clock) and using it to construct a means of transport or pathway to avoid an obstruction. There are points available for speed as well as efficiency.
- **Outward bound.** Individuals or teams tackle physically demanding tasks in the open air with the aim of exploring attitudes to risk, teamwork and physical hardship. Surviving a night in open country or rock climbing are just two examples. Recently this type of activity has had mixed reviews, with the suggestion that it is actually demotivating for staff to

discover their manager cannot read a map or suffers from vertigo. You need to be clear about your objectives and be aware of the potential downside ('I didn't join the bank to risk my life down a pothole'). Safety is a key criterion when selecting an activity.

- **Sports.** For particular groups who would be entertained by trying out different sports (archery, snooker, golf, clay-pigeon shooting, tennis, croquet, crossbow, bowls, car rallying, buggy driving, driving a fire engine, ballooning: the list is endless). Once again what you like may not be what your guests would like, particularly if partners are to be invited, so offer alternatives.
- **National sporting events.** A common interim award in many motivation programmes is a ticket to a national sporting event. The growth of corporate hospitality packages to the Olympics, horse racing events and the like is testimony to their popularity. However, it is important to retain ownership of the hosting element. All too often winners can remember what event they attended, but not who paid for it or what the achievement was. Whenever possible, book private facilities so the sponsors can take full credit for providing the reward in the first place.

Choosing the right activity for the right people is an art and can gel or split a group, depending on their willingness or otherwise to participate. In general, go carefully if it is a group of winners and their partners. An optional approach might be best so that those with a health problem can opt out and not feel pressurized, while others may simply not want to 'participate' with strangers so you need to be accommodating. Staff or singles are easier in that they generally want to participate, but take care to cater for all tastes. For example, if a two-day teamwork reward relies heavily on golf, non-golfing participants may feel discriminated against.

STAFF PARTIES

Although discretionary staff events such as the Christmas party, family fun days, new office openings, company anniversaries or

other corporate events are not strictly part of a motivation programme, they are part of a motivational mindset. We have all
noticed at one time or another the discrepancy in quality
between events for the sales force as an incentive and an event
organized by the company to mark some corporate occasion for
staff. Treating all staff with the same degree of sensitivity and
courtesy is a motivational issue. As part of the motivational mix,
internal corporate events should be handled by professionals, be
allocated a meaningful budget and have specific objectives. The
benefit of an overall incentive programme or a profit-share
scheme can be totally undone by a penny-pinching approach to
staff events.

In broad terms building loyalty, and establishing a reward and
recognition culture for staff as well as sales people, needs careful
attention to detail if the investment is going to pay off in the long
term in terms of staff retention and the internal willingness to
share best practice techniques.

Events are important

Participants may or may not have had to qualify for conferences
or events, but even if they are not strictly incentives or rewards,
they still present an opportunity to nurture a 'we can do better'
attitude. By accepting the fact that company events are part of the
motivational mix, you are building staff or distributor loyalty for
some time in the future when you may need their complete support. If you fail to input quality for internal events (or interim
campaigns in the case of an overall incentive programme), you
may not get the quality output from staff when you need it most.
In blunt terms, you either care or you don't.

Research staff response

Like all other marketing activities, staff events should be com-
petently researched so that you can be sure that you are producing appropriate events. Organizing activities that staff feel
embarrassed to attend is not only a waste of resources but

detrimental to corporate morale. Listen carefully to what staff say about centrally organized events and, within the relevant budget constraints, try to deliver what they would enjoy.

SUMMARY

- Events can be a powerful way to strengthen the motivational mix.
- Conferences in particular can resolve complex morale problems.
- Weekend incentives need just as much attention to detail as large overseas groups.
- Non-incentive related staff events should be as high quality as performance-related events.

---

11 Measure, monitor, mirror

Mirror, mirror on the wall, who is the fairest of them all?
The Black Queen in *Snow White*

Now that the reward choices are clear, the next step is to consider how to measure performance, because someone, somewhere is bound to ask, sooner or later, whether the investment has paid off. The three stages in this process happen to alliterate which makes them easy to remember:

1. Measure – establish the performance standard.
2. Monitor – calculate how each individual or group is doing.
3. Mirror – tell the participants the results.

Of all the decisions you may make when constructing a motivation programme, establishing the criteria for performance improvement is usually the least attractive but the most important task. Without robust measures, you will never know whether it has all been worth the trouble.

Quality control
Operating standards manifest themselves in many ways. From the legal accounting procedures of auditors to keeping an eye on

the daily receipt of incoming orders, all managers rely on some form of performance reporting so they can gauge how well or badly their department, the company or the market is doing.

The modern quality standards discipline has a distinguished past, from the famous Hawthorne experiments of Elton Mayo, which first suggested that man expects more than solely economic gains to be a satisfied worker, to the Total Quality Management principles of Taylor and Deming and their disciples. The introduction of customer service strategies and recognized quality standards is an expression of the awakening of this need for more accountability when it comes to measuring staff performance.

But how relevant are these measures to real people doing real jobs? Can so-called non-producing administrative functions ever be measured effectively? They can and they are. But before we start the benchmarking process we need to establish why support staff need measuring at all, apart from the occasional, usually annual, heart-to-heart with their manager.

Why bother to measure support staff?

For many years quality, particularly in service industries, has been both a necessity and an annoyance. With such an elusive objective – quality – it seems to many management teams that achieving superior quality is just a question of investing more money in product development than their rivals. Promotion helps to establish the new 'quality' product, but if you rely on administration or production teams to produce it, all that development and promotion could be wasted. When the customer eventually comes face to face with the product or service, if support staff do not reinforce the new quality image then the consumer feels 'cognitive dissonance' ('Did I do the right thing by buying this product?'). The more expensive the product, such as a car or a pension plan, the more uncertain the consumer becomes. Supporting the quality product with a quality infrastructure is a vital ingredient in securing the sale, not just for now but for any repeat sales.

A quality approach to human resources ensures that expectations are met and that the promise is delivered.

MEASURE

With any group of people, you need to decide four fundamental questions when preparing an incentive scheme or performance-improvement programme:

1. What elements of performance should be measured?
2. How can they be measured?
3. Will successful achievement deliver meaningful financial benefits?
4. Are the data both fair and robust?

1. Elements of performance

In Chapter 3 we considered a variety of business objectives that could be addressed, for both sales and non-sales groups, through performance improvement programmes. But now we have to bite the bullet and say what exactly we are going to measure. All measurements start with an initial standard from which future improvements can be gauged. The first task, therefore, is to set a standard.

Individual job performance is a complex combination of many tasks, some more important than others. In a non-sales or supportive environment you may need to think long and hard about what performance standards you can measure. In a typical administrative job there will be a core of functions that constitute adequate performance:

- timekeeping, attendance;
- telephone skills;
- keyboard skills;
- clerical accuracy, numeracy.

All these functions can be easily measured either objectively or by the supervisor. But beyond these basic skills there is a raft of other attributes that make an average employee into a high flyer, regardless of the job grade. Here are some examples:

- problem solving;
- general 'can do' attitude;
- positive response to deadlines/peaks and troughs;
- team player;
- leadership potential;
- task orientation;
- willingness to learn new skills.

These skills are inherently more subjective but can be vital to establishing a relevant standard. All of them can be measured either by the supervisor or by the individual's peers, on a simple scale of 1 to 10 for any given period.

However, the important thing is to decide which of the many elements constitute the core performance criteria for that job. For instance, a service engineer working for a national power utility carries out specific core behaviour patterns which can be regularly monitored, even though the engineer may not be constantly supervised:

- attendance;
- percentage of customer visits made on time;
- percentage of problems solved;
- error-free paperwork;
- additional sales.

You may wish to add a supervisor's category to award credits for general attitude or some other team-player type of attribute. But if in doubt, particularly if you feel favouritism could play a part, stick to known behaviour patterns you can measure objectively.

Junior staff

A junior administrator working in a credit-card company could have measurable job functions as follows:

- speed of keying in;
- accuracy of keying in;
- average length of customer telephone query;

- additional services sold to customers;
- timekeeping.

A team-player factor could be added, where peers vote each month for the person in their group who has gone beyond the call of duty to deliver customer satisfaction, although the weighting for this element should not be as high as for the objective elements, to ensure fair play and factor out potential supervisor bias.

Senior staff

Even senior managers can be set standards which can be objectively scrutinized, although they tend to be more to do with specific financial or quality controls:

- retention rates of staff;
- expenditure control;
- regular reports delivered on time;
- use of training support for staff;
- evidence of regular team communication.

Once established, the core behaviour standards need not necessarily be written in stone. In many industries technology is moving so fast the key constituents of good performance could change overnight, or the company may need to stimulate a specific approach to customer service. This would lead to redefining the key standards on which to base any performance improvement process. In practice the assessment of basic standards should be carried out at least once a year, if only to check that the measures are all still meaningful. There are many examples of a mature scheme producing such high standards in one area (attendance, clerical errors, telephone manner) that continued emphasis is wasteful. The measure has reached its optimum, which means that it is time to examine other elements of the process.

Autoglass improves internal standards

Autoglass is one of Europe's leading car window replacement companies. Some years ago Autoglass embarked on a performance improvement programme for all its 2,000 staff. After considerable analysis of job types and historical performance patterns, staff were categorized as belonging to one of four key areas: distribution, central control (telesales), head office and branches.

Each job task was analysed to identify specific areas of performance improvement, such as customer service, errors in distribution, clerical mistakes and repairs achieved. An historical standard was set for each task and the ensuing improvements were measured for the first time. Rewards in the form of retail vouchers, rather than the traditional cash bonus, were introduced for individual achievement over and above the stated standard.

Performance improved significantly in many areas:

- The number of 'abandoned' calls (customers who hang up) fell from 3.5 per cent to just 1 per cent.
- The average number of clerical errors in customer documentation fell from 20 per cent to 5 per cent.
- Customer complaints fell from 12 per cent to 7.5 per cent.
- The Customer Opinion Index rose significantly.

The programme enabled Autoglass to move from a customer-reactive organization to a customer service business, with a substantial increase in its customers' perception of it as a reliable, service-oriented company.

Once you have decided what relevant elements to measure, the next task is to measure them.

2. How practical is it to measure performance elements?

With infinite resources, everything is measurable. However, there comes a point when the cost of gathering the data outweighs the incremental benefit. It may be perfectly feasible to analyse the job descriptions of 10,000 staff, establish their key tasks, brief managers and peers, award points for successful completion, and issue everyone with an individual rating each month against the average achievement. But the cost would be enormous and too time consuming. It may be best to decide which

Table 11.1   Motivation programme participation plans

Employee category	Specific programme
Directors	✗
Sales	✔
Marketing	✗
Administration	✗
Production	✗
Distribution	✔

✗ = non-participation, ✔ = participation.

elements of the performance mix would deliver the greatest incremental benefit to the company, if detailed performance measures were introduced.

Let us take an example. An IT company has many categories of contributor to the process of creating profit. (See Table 11.1.)

Clearly, in theory, all categories would benefit from a performance improvement process if the company is going to be successful. But with scarce resources it may be that by concentrating on sales (new business) and distribution (delivering the product) the available resources can produce rapid incremental benefits, providing enough profits to bring others into the loop at some later stage.

Total Quality Management consultants may argue that everyone should be involved in the reorientation process. In theory, this is correct. Attitudes are important, right down the line, but if the choice is to do nothing because the company cannot afford a fully integrated scheme at present, it is better for everyone to do something. Performance improvement is the art of the practical rather than the science of following rigid theories.

Once you have decided which categories to concentrate on, you will have another choice. Which elements of current job performance can be measured now, without any investment in data collection or new reporting systems? Many companies embarking on performance improvement for the first time are surprised to learn that they already have the measurement systems in place. The trick is to reorganize the data so that they can be played back to the employees in a format they will understand. Administrative functions often have a multitude of performance measures known only to management. By communicating what these measures are (and what constitutes success in the eyes of the managers), the staff suddenly become aware of the real 'rules of the game'. It is difficult to score a goal if the goalposts are always shrouded in fog. Usually, the eventual measures to be used turn out to be a mixture of existing measures and a few new measures emphasizing a specific operational issue. Together, the new overall standard forms the starting point for relevant performance improvement.

3. Delivering benefits

Before we set off down the golden road of perfect performance, we need to be a little wary of creating flawless behaviour but no profit. Each improvement should have a financial rationale. Keeping the office tidy is a worthy performance improvement but is unlikely to produce any major financial benefit. Improving sales prospecting activity, producing more efficient keyboard personnel and creating fewer clerical errors can all be calculated in financial terms as producing a quantifiable benefit. It is true that 'better teamwork' or displaying a 'can do' attitude cannot be objectively measured in scientific terms, so with some measures a certain leap of faith is required. But whenever possible, underpin any choice of measures with a cost/benefit analysis.

Telesales performance improvement

The number of dial spins (successful connections to a prospect's place of work or home) by a telesales person per month is directly proportional to the number of appointments made. If we can increase dial spins by 20 per cent in a given period, we will increase appointments made by 20 per cent. The normal ratio of appointments to sales can be calculated and hence the incremental revenue.

In other words, the incentive produced five sales instead of four, so the extra revenue generated was £15,000. (See Table 11.2.)

Table 11.2 Ratios of appointments to sales and calculated revenue

	Dial spins	Appointments	Sales	Revenue
Without programme	200	10	4	£60,000
With programme	240	12	5	£75,000
Incremental revenue				£15,000

Administration performance improvement

The percentage of breakages by a warehouse staff is directly proportional to the warehouse operating overhead. If we can reduce breakages from 10 to 5 per cent, we can reduce the operating costs of the distribution function. (See Table 11.3.)

Table 11.3 Effect of breakages on replacement costs

	Breakages	Replacement cost
Without programme	10%	£50,000
With programme	5%	£25,000
Incremental saving		£25,000

Each example will be different. In many cases you may have to make an educated guess about the level of improvement (it depends on the professionalism of the performance improvement programme). However, in most cases, companies underestimate the improvements actually gained and are pleasantly surprised by the eventual benefits.

4. Robust data

One final element in setting the initial benchmark is to ensure the data are robust. In other words, is the information you are collecting credible? The more subjective the measure, the more likely it can be corrupted through bias. If it is a key measure on which an individual's or a group's performance depends, the whole programme may be undermined. Collection of the data needs also to be constant. If, for example, a monthly performance measure is a factor of three separate measures, what happens if one of those measures is not available? Do you use the two measures that have come in and ignore the absence of the third measure? Do you substitute the missing measure with an historic weighted average? Do you exclude that individual or team from the process completely that month? These problems need to be thought through before the programme is launched. If in doubt, remove that unreliable measure before you start.

By examining all these issues before establishing the initial measures to be used, you will find the monitoring and communication process much easier.

MONITOR

The monitoring process covers how performance data are to be collected during each measurement period so that change can be shown. It is a data management discipline which requires professional computer knowledge and logical routines.

Depending on the sources of data (one office, regional offices, suppliers, market surveys) and the format of the data (manual, diskettes, modem), the periodic data collection task can either be simple or very complex indeed. In an ideal world a single modem download from one source drives the report. In practice this is rarely the case. Most company data systems are driven by payroll routines or production processes, so adapting the current system to provide data for performance improvement programmes is never straightforward. The most practical solution is to write a separate program which can receive the data in the inevitable variety of formats.

Typical participant profile fields

To ensure that performance data about two separate participants do not get mixed up or misposted, we need to establish some unique characteristics for each individual record:

- first name initial;
- surname;
- employment joining date;
- employee number;
- employee job title;
- employee job grade;
- location address;
- full or part-time;
- employment leaving date (if relevant).

With 50 participants this could be done manually. With 5,000 participants, it would be impossible to keep track manually of every Mr Smith who joined, then left, then joined again as a part-timer. If individual performance ratings are going to be communicated it is vital to identify the right Mr Smith.

Typical performance fields

To assess change we need to track where we are now with where we were the last time we analysed the data. For example:

- target;
- target achievement comparison;
- number of transactions;
- attendance percentage;
- quality threshold achievement;
- documentation error rate;
- items processed against target;
- customer survey assessment;
- supervisor's rating.

Each individual will have a different matrix of performance measures. Those who belong to different job grades or regions may well be performing against different numerical criteria.

Administration skills

Those who have the job of collecting and merging all these data need to have specific file import routines, otherwise no one will ever be able to unravel the various sources (and dates) of data imported. The process is a mechanical one with no scope for deviation, but the more data can be merged electronically without 'human' intervention, the better.

Assuming both manual and electronic data have been gathered we can then progress to probably the most important aspect of a performance improvement campaign – telling participants how they are doing.

MIRROR

Output is where the whole exercise becomes meaningful. Without regular information about changes in individual or team performance, there is no programme and there will be no sustained improvement. Participants need to be told how they are doing. Moreover, sponsors need to know whether their investment is paying off.

To mirror back performance there are many media to choose from.

- **Letter.** A personalized letter can be produced, driven by the main software program, to show individual performance against the key tasks laid out during the launch of the campaign. It could contain one element of data – sales achievement against target – or several performance measures, depending on the complexity of the programme.
- **Bulletin.** Normally used for incentives, the same information can be dramatized and highlighted using computer graphics, overprinted on preprinted stationery or delivered as a screen graphic. A skier going down a slalom with flags denoting percentage achievement of target, a galleon sailing around an island or a car racing to the chequered flag can all enhance the performance message, and help participants identify what they have to do to improve.
- **Wallposters.** Depending on the cultural environment of the workplace, rank order positions or achievement against prescribed job tasks can be displayed as a wallposter so that peer

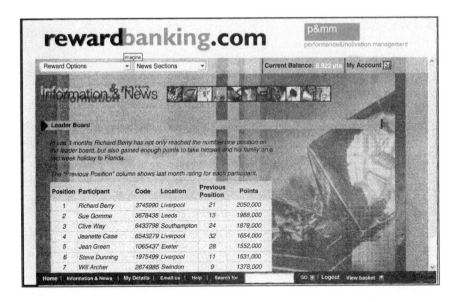

Figure 11.1   Rewardbanking leader board

group pressure starts to work on those not pulling their weight, especially if it is a team-based incentive.

- **E-mails.** For immediacy, performance can be 'called up' on desktop information screens at will or sent as 'must read' messages. This approach allows the organizer to respond very quickly to performance improvements, allowing participants to discover the effect of their achievement as quickly as possible after the behaviour change.

- **Regular magazine.** To enhance the importance of any improvements made, a more permanent format is a regular magazine which can highlight faces as well as names and carry interviews with 'top improvers'. As internet and intranet technology advance an online desktop magazine will be a powerful motivational tool for reinforcing mid-campaign improvements and creating role models within each peer group.

Figure 11.1 shows an example of a simple leader board, taken from the Rewardbanking website featured in Chapter 9.

As you can see, points are shown for the current month and a ranked position established. In addition the list also shows what position participants were in the previous month, so they can see what progress has been made.

Whichever medium is chosen, response times are a major factor in closing the loop between achievement and recognition of achievement. Programmes that launch well but have no mid-campaign follow-through in terms of performance monitoring are not only less effective but wasteful of the initial investment.

Local management involvement

As for most central initiatives within a large company, local management needs to be consulted about the style and timing of the performance communication so that they can support the central message locally. They will need, in addition, to be sent detailed management reports about the performance of their own people, compared with the national or grade average, so that they can take corrective action or indeed publicly praise those team members who are performing well (see Chapter 9).

Setting relevant measures and being able to report to participants on their progress is what distinguishes a performance improvement campaign from a sales promotion. Most employees deserve more than just a short-term bribe, if you are serious about creating sustainable changes in the way a company goes about the process of creating added value

---

SUMMARY

- Setting the initial measures needs to be done in the context of what is practical.
- Monitoring the progress of individuals or teams will help participants to work even harder.
- Communication of performance during the programme needs to be as close as possible in time to the achievement.
- Involve local management so they can support local performance improvements.

12

Recognition systems

Applauding success and forgiving failure ...

Charles Handy

No reward without recognition. No recognition without reward. In the first instance the sponsor misses a big opportunity by not squeezing out the last ounce of publicity and acknowledgement while in the act of bestowing a reward. In the latter case, recognizing good performance without rewarding it will be perceived as cheap and cynical by most workforces. Every participant knows how inexpensive it is to produce a certificate.

By itself, a recognition system is often the poor relation in many performance improvement programmes. It is either an afterthought to the main activity of constructing the campaign, or it replaces part of the campaign when budgets are cut. Recognition systems only work when they are integrated into the main programme. They grease the wheels and transform an average programme into an incremental profit earner for very little extra budget. It is rarely acknowledged that recognition is, in fact, a type of reward. Repeated employee surveys consistently show that one of an employee's most highly rated needs at work is to receive recognition for a job well done. Yet, according to Kouzes and Posner (1998)[1], 40 per cent of workers claim that they have never received recognition for outstanding individual performance.

But what are recognition systems and why are they so important?

WHY RECOGNITION WORKS

If we revisit motivational theory, we can see several ideas tending towards the same conclusion.

- Maslow's hierarchy of needs[2] describes a level of need where belonging to a peer group and distinguishing oneself in a specific skill within that peer group is a basic human urge.
- Henry Murray cites two of his Twenty Basic Needs[3] as: 'To rival and surpass others.... To increase self-regard by successful exercise of talent.'
- Cottrell in 'Social facilitation'[4] argues, 'when two or more people act together the intensity of their individual behaviour often increases'.

If we can supply something to feed these basic urges, performance will increase. Corporate recognition systems do just that.

TYPES OF CORPORATE RECOGNITION

Beyond the basic level of corporate survival, loosely termed as holding down a job, what drives comfort-zone employees on is recognition by their superiors and their peers. Recognition comes in many media, both formal and informal:

- memo from an immediate superior;
- letter from 'the boss' (divisional director, managing director, chairperson);
- certificate denoting technical competence;
- certificate denoting above-average competence;
- trophy for top achievement;

- lunch or dinner with superiors;
- discretionary reward for extraordinary performance;
- story in the company newsletter or magazine;
- private verbal 'well done' by telephone or face to face;
- public recognition of achievement in front of peers;
- public, industry recognition of individual achievement;
- national industry award for individual or group performance;
- lapel pins and badges.

Within every performance improvement programme there will be scope to arrange things in such a way that many of the above ways to recognize achievement can be built into the programme.

Chevron brings out the best

Even experienced companies can learn from their mistakes in using recognition schemes. Some years ago Chevron Chemical conducted a routine survey of its five-year-old recognition programme, only to discover that more than 50 per cent of the participants felt that supervisors had too much say in who got recognized. Nominations were put forward to a management committee, who then decided among themselves who received the awards.

The scheme was overhauled actively to exclude the supervisory layer and have no management input whatsoever. The new programme, called 'Bringing Out The Best', was simplified to cut down on expensive internal administration at the same time. Employees could now recognize any good practice contributions by fellow employees by completing a short three-part form, the bottom section of which was a points voucher that could be redeemed for a wide range of awards. To maintain the quality of the recognition scheme, each employee was given only six vouchers for distribution per year, but there was no limit on the number of awards that any one person could receive. In addition, awards could be given to anyone in the organization by anyone in the organization. The CEO could get one from the mailroom, if he or she were deserving enough.

Over 79 per cent of employees gave out three or more certificates in the first year of operation of the new scheme, and over 90 per cent of the workforce considered it to be good or very good so far as participant research was concerned, citing the 'instant' feature of recognition for a job well done as a significant improvement over the original programme.

CLUB CONCEPTS

Within corporate incentive schemes, club concepts not only increase loyalty but provide many ways to recognize above-average performance. But what do we mean by a 'club concept'?

Consumer 'clubs' have been around for many years with the aim of selling additional products to established customers with the propensity to buy. Book clubs are the obvious example. Any list of past and present customers can be consolidated into a club concept. The fabric of the club is usually held together via direct marketing techniques: a newsletter or magazine is the normal medium. Club concepts for staff or distribution networks are somewhat different, depending on how close the sponsor is to the potential members. For employed or self-employed sales people a club is usually a structured annual incentive programme comprising a single big travel event at the end of the year, supported by shorter-term tactical promotion during the year. Club membership is determined by achievement of a specific sales or quality threshold which triggers access to a variety of club benefits. Many can be simply 'hygiene factor' items (for example free parking at head office, fast-track administration, participation in the company staff issues meeting). Other benefits can be related directly to doing more business (free use of a laptop computer, secretarial services, appointment-making service). The third group of benefits tends to cover recognition elements such as cufflinks, brooches, ties, ladies' scarves, certificates and trophies for the top qualifiers.

A financial services club concept

Most insurance companies that operate sales forces that sell direct to consumers have some kind of sales club. Aimed at the top 25 per cent, specific thresholds of commission are set to divide the qualifying participants into tiers to instil loyalty, improve retention and provide peer group recognition opportunities. Often no additional remuneration is paid, but there are significant non-cash benefits offered:

- invitation to the annual sales conference;
- invitation to the prestigious travel incentive destination;
- gold, silver or bronze cufflinks;
- tie denoting gold, silver or bronze membership;
- certificate of achievement;
- specific editorial in the sales force magazine.

Communication to the sales force in total or to individuals always includes reference to their club status, and rank-order tables of achievement are produced and distributed on a regular basis during the sales year, not only to recognize past achievement but also to stimulate would-be qualifiers to qualify the following year.

DISTRIBUTOR CLUBS

Distributor clubs are characterized by contribution, in the same way as for sales forces. Depending on purchases made from the manufacturer, individual dealers or stockists benefit from preferential joint marketing programmes or invitations to specific manufacturer-sponsored events, by virtue of the turnover generated.

Carl Zeiss Italiana

In Italy, the Carl Zeiss Club recognizes target achievement among independent optical stockists, and supports the Zeiss brand image of high prestige and traditional values. There are three levels of membership – member, honorary member and VIP – and varying levels of recognition. VIP members, for example, receive a silver membership card in a leather holder, which acts as a credit card to 'purchase' items from the Club Secretariat (a selection of merchandise and leisure services). In addition, VIP members qualify for a prestigious event with partners (Monte Carlo, Venice, Capri) restricted to the top 40 stockists. So sought-after has the Carl Zeiss Club become that some stockists feature their membership in their consumer outlets and advertising.

It is often difficult to prove that such recognition devices produce more incremental profit. The only way to do so would be to divide the target market in half and offer the benefits to one side only. However, it always makes sound commercial sense to concentrate your efforts on those most likely to support your products. Most 'clubs' are aimed at the top echelon of distributors because their loyalty can help you to build market share more quickly than by attempting to be 'fair' to everyone.

FREQUENT BUYER/LOYALTY PROGRAMMES

Taking the business commitment logic further down the road to true market representation, frequent buyer or channel loyalty programmes tie in the producer and the distribution arm even more closely. When buyers purchase up to specified levels, credits are generated in a centrally held marketing fund to support joint or independent local marketing activity.

Epson

Epson was the world leader in printers but it needed to raise its profile in the United Kingdom. It realized it could not outspend IBM in marketing initiatives, but it could generate loyalty from a selected group of UK dealers. A quality standards programme was set up in which dealers could earn credits through achieving specific Epson-related performance standards in such elements as showroom, use of merchandising material, staff product knowledge and handling supplied advertising leads from Epson. The credits gained could be exchanged for a wide range of business support services including direct mail, local advertising, exhibition display materials, marketing consultancy, and attendance at international IT conferences and exhibitions.

INFORMAL RECOGNITION

One of the hardest techniques to master is informal recognition, very often the most effective loyalty builder. In the industrialized West, particularly in Europe, formal recognition systems can be perceived by staff as an alternative to increasing remuneration and a cheap way of buying loyalty. After all, everyone can see that a few certificates and a lunch with the boss cost much less than a pay increase across the board. If this is the prevailing attitude, a recognition programme will do more harm than good. It may be worth stepping back from the morale problem, and examining how managers go about blaming and praising staff.

A workshop can be devised to outline the basic psychology of supervisor/supervised relationships and agree a series of informal recognition techniques to build internal confidence and morale. Once the management and staff are communicating effectively in this way, more formal systems can be grafted on top as a natural expression of the new culture.

Recognition systems are not an inexpensive panacea for poor morale. Staff can spot an insincere management attitude instantly. So such initiatives need to be treated with care and used in conjunction with other incentive, reward and performance techniques if they are going to be received at face value.

Club concepts are so widespread that some incentive agencies have set up specific departments to deal with club organization for corporate clients. Bernard Krief Motivation, France, sells a 'club kit' to companies that want the loyalty but not the administration a club can generate. Through careful collection of members' data, a series of offers are developed to appeal to particular member types to ensure there is always a basic financial benefit of membership in addition to any client product loyalty. The club kit costs a modest amount per person per year, including special deals and regular communication. But it always depends on the particular brief and the frequency of contact required.

William James, the 19th-century philosopher, wrote, 'The deepest principle in human nature is the craving to be appreciated.' The message about recognition systems is that by giving people what they want (more appreciation in the workplace) they will give you what you want: better commitment and higher productivity.

SUMMARY

- No reward without recognition. No recognition without reward.
- Feed the basic need to be recognized for doing well.
- Club concepts increase loyalty and help build corporate relationships.
- Frequent buyer programmes help to fund joint marketing initiatives.
- Develop informal recognition habits.
- Integrate recognition schemes into wider performance improvement programmes to get the best results.

---

1 Kouzes, James M and Posner, Barry Z (1998) *Encouraging the Heart: A leader's guide to rewarding and recognizing others,* Jossey-Bass, San Francisco.
2 Maslow, A (1943) 'A theory of human motivation' in Psychological Review, 50, 370–396.
3 Murray, H A (1938) *Explorations in Personality,* Oxford University Press, New York.
4 Cottrell, N B (1972) 'Social facilitation' in *Experimental Social Psychology,* ed C G McClintock, Holt, Rinehart & Winston, New York.

13

The future of incentives

Development is always self-development.... The responsibility rests with the individual, his abilities, his efforts.

Peter Drucker

As in every other aspect of business life, the internet has made and will continue to make a considerable impact on the way businesses improve their performance in the marketplace, and by implication on the performance of their people. Better efficiencies and higher ratios go hand in hand with faster data and quicker analysis of the ever-changing market picture.

Using the performance improvement model outlined in Chapter 3 as our guide to what the future could look like, interaction in all four areas of research, skills, communication and incentives will be more prominent. When we research staff attitudes or distributor communication, information will be posted on an intranet, providing virtually instant feedback on what participants think. Real-time telemetry – measuring people from a distance – is now a reality. The days are almost gone when you had to wait until the end of the campaign before assessing its success rate. With virtual contact between participants, the programme sponsor and the organizing agency (if there is one), misunderstandings can be ironed out within a matter of days, and the scheme made more appropriate as the weeks go by rather than having to let it run its course because 'the brochures have already been printed'.

Probably the swiftest to change will be the area of skills development. Many training organizations are already reducing the time and expense of sending staff on external courses and opting for distance learning or home-based tutoring packages instead. At the moment these are mostly on CD ROMs, but within a few years there is no doubt that the standard way to learn a new skill will be online with access to a 'live' tutor. Assessment will be instant and staff will simply log on to the required module if a new skill is needed. Because of the pressure on efficiency it is likely that such training will be done at home or while travelling once WAP technology and the various reception devices are robust enough. Traditionalists will say that you cannot teach management skills through a PC screen. That may be true, but such high-level training is only a small part of the whole range of skills development that people need to do a better job. It seems inevitable that more than 90 per cent of all skills training in business will be remote from now on.

The worldwide internet revolution has all been based on better communications, whether we are considering private individuals or B2B (business-to-business). Within the context of incentive schemes the revolution has already started, with many campaigns having their own website, being launched virtually (there is no glossy brochure) and with participants being able to check their performance on a daily basis on-screen from home or work rather than having to wait for the monthly bulletin. The extra dimension that instant communication brings is the ability to redeem rewards without delay, thereby achieving one of the great theoretical goals of sound motivation: being rewarded as close to the changed behaviour as possible, so as to reinforce it. There is still the problem of delivering items of merchandise, but at least the time lags are improving now that suppliers know more quickly what will be required and when.

As for the rewards themselves, there will be increasing emphasis on personal travel or experience-related products as people become relatively more affluent and simply do not need essential domestic merchandise or cash-substitutes as an award when they can have whatever it is supplied locally, probably at a much cheaper price. Participants will be more inclined to accumulate their points for something memorable and less transient or mundane. There is also a trend towards involving family and friends in awards in the form of subsidized weekends or holidays, or even part-funding of a family celebration. Printed merchandise catalogues may well be on the way out, as winners opt for more individually tailored redemption options they can choose from the comfort of their own PC with the involvement of their family. The better reward systems are now keeping track of participant preferences and even being proactive in suggesting what type of reward would be appropriate via the campaign website as specific reward levels are achieved.

Another aspect that may change is the nature of the consultancy advice that is offered. Until quite recently sales-related programmes dominated performance improvement schemes wherever they were undertaken. Estimates of 80 per cent sales, 20 per cent non-sales would not be far wrong. But with the shift towards consumers buying direct and internet companies providing services on the end of a telephone line or a radio wave, the big growth area has to be in staff schemes. Improving performance at work to be more customer-oriented, more knowledgeable about products, more numerate, more flexible and more communicative is certainly something all organizations need. Programmes to improve internal processes and become more efficient and more customer-friendly will need to be managed with sensitivity and thoroughness as more and more people opt to work part-time or even from their own homes. The new model for a successful business does not necessarily include bricks and mortar or having a large national administration centre any more.

Employees are changing too. People are no longer content just to eke out their working hours until it is time to go home. They ask for more involvement, more information, more control and more personally relevant performance-related rewards. They want to be involved in the process of creating value. They want to be recognized for having done a good job more than once a year in a formal appraisal. They want to be thanked and they want it now. When they get that involvement the improvement in the daily operations of a business can be remarkable. But their reward should not simply be more money, for the reasons we have already discussed. There is a distinct advantage to be harvested from looking at cost-effective non-cash, tangible options, being critical about the internal communication of job performance, and investing in an organization's biggest asset – its people.

Encourage participation

In this brief guide I have tried to examine how a team leader, a manager or even a CEO can bring out the potential in every individual to improve performance at work. Not all the techniques described will work for you. There is no magic formula that will be effective at all levels and for all types of organization. Cultures are different. Markets are constantly changing. You need to experiment to discover what works in your situation.

But above all, you need to let ordinary workers participate in the improvement process. People do have the capacity to respond and change, sometimes in spite of what the organization says or does. Only by taking on a personal responsibility for improving the performance of your people and your own performance will you be able to reap the rewards. Your job, as a 'motivational interventionist' is to facilitate that process.

Index